DISCARD

Y0-BLT-379

R0l030 36815

```
LC          Carrasquillo,
225.3         Angela.
.C37
1993        Parents and schools.
```

$38.00

DATE			

CHICAGO PUBLIC LIBRARY
SOCIAL SCIENCES AND HISTORY
400 S. STATE ST.   60605

BAKER & TAYLOR

PARENTS AND SCHOOLS

SOURCE BOOKS ON EDUCATION
(VOL. 37)

GARLAND REFERENCE LIBRARY
OF SOCIAL SCIENCE
(VOL. 775)

PARENTS AND SCHOOLS
A Source Book

Angela L. Carrasquillo
Clement B. G. London

GARLAND PUBLISHING, INC. • NEW YORK & LONDON
1993

© 1993 Angela L. Carrasquillo and Clement B. G. London
All rights reserved

Library of Congress Cataloging-in-Publication Data

Carrasquillo, Angela.
    Parents and schools : a source book / Angela L.
Carrasquillo, Clement B. G. London.
       p. cm. — (Garland reference library of social science ;
vol. 775. Source books on education ; vol. 37)
    Includes bibliographical references and index.
    ISBN 0-8153-0820-5
    1. Home and school—United States. 2. Home and school—
United States—Cross-cultural studies. 3. Education—United
States—Parent participation. 4. Education—United States—
Parent participation—Cross-cultural studies. 5. Parent and
child—United States. I. London, Clement B. G. II. Title.
III. Series: Garland reference library of social science ; v. 775.
IV. Series: Garland reference library of social science ; v. 775.
Source books on education ; v. 37.
LC225.3.C37 1993
649-'.68—dc20   92-6699
                                                                                    CIP

Printed on acid-free, 250-year-life paper
Manufactured in the United States of America

CONTENTS

Preface	vii
Introduction	ix
Chapter 1 U.S. Families in the Context of Change	3
Chapter 2 The African-American Experience in Family Context	13
Chapter 3 The Hispanic-American Experience in Family Context	35
Chapter 4 The Asian-American Experience in Family Context	51
Chapter 5 Communities of Education	69
Chapter 6 Empowerment for All Parents	97
Chapter 7 Required: A Positive Self-Concept	113

Chapter 8
    Successful Schools: A Parents and Educators'
    Partnership   141

Chapter 9
    Successful Students: Ability, Effort, and
    Parental Involvement   159

Chapter 10
    Parents: First and Most Important Teachers   175

Chapter 11
    Recommendations for the Improvement of
    Parental School Involvement   207

Chapter 12
    Advocacy for School and Home Partnership   219

Author Index   233

Subject Index   239

PREFACE

This book focuses on the hypothesis that both the school and the parents need to see themselves as partners working hand in hand for the social, emotional, cognitive, and academic development of their students and their children. The school needs to provide a strong leadership model, a healthy classroom climate, and staff that foster learning. Parents need to see themselves as reinforcers of learning and as vital instruments in their children's education. Schools and parents need to understand the necessity for increased participation on their part, so that efforts will be reflected in tangible forms, such as improved attendance at school and progress in academic performance.

This book presents the school/parent relationship with enthusiasm. The authors emphasize throughout the book that parents and educators need to celebrate the pleasure of teaching. For this reason there are chapters on successful schools and successful students, as well as on successful parents and successful teachers. As parents and educators become more involved in successful school programs and with successful students, they recognize a need for greater self-improvement. Closer contact with the schools will motivate parents to seek more schooling for themselves as a means of improvement. Through the increased involvement of parents, school personnel will experience greater degrees of success among their student bodies. The parents' input will generate a more relevant educational plan, one that is based on the specific needs and characteristics of the school population. The joint partnership between parents and educators will enhance the multicultural and multilingual nature of our society and the responsibility that schools have to their students.

The content of the book should interest a wide range of educators, parents, and community organizations, as well as all those who are concerned with the well-being of children and youth. The book can be used as a primary or a secondary source in courses on parenting, parental involvement, human relations, staff development, and change processes in schools. In-service specialists will find relevant information in the book on planning and implementing successful relationships between schools and parents and community organizations. This book is a good guide for parents and community organizations or community advocacy groups in understanding the meaning of partnerships between school and community.

We wish to thank those individuals who helped us prepare this book; above all, those parents and their children who inspired us to write about the many components involved in developing successful schools and parental partnerships. We also thank our students at Fordham University who provided us with the forum to conceptualize the content of this book. Lourdes Willems diligently typed the manuscript. The support and encouragement of our spouses—Ceferino Carrasquillo and Pearl London—as well as of our children were invaluable in the writing of this book.

Angela L. Carrasquillo
Clement B. G. London

INTRODUCTION

Traditionally, parents have been expected to delegate the responsibility for educating their children to teachers and the school. Because this approach has failed to produce the kinds of educational programs that meet the needs of many of today's students, the current trend has been to perceive the school primarily as part of the local community and the parental support system. Consequently, parents and educators are recognizing the importance of active parental and community participation; and federal- and state-sponsored programs are mandating this type of involvement. The concept of increased parental and community involvement has been incorporated in most educational programs.

Research on parental involvement in education indicates that the alterable curriculum of the home as well as the teaching home is twice as predictive of academic learning as is family socioeconomic status (Burke, 1990; Chavkin, 1989; Dulney, 1987). Moreover, besides the value-added component of a strong relationship between parental involvement and student achievement, there are other related benefits. Among these benefits are such factors as the lowering of barriers to family participation in the schools, increased student attendance, decreased drop-out rate, positive parent-child communications, improvement of student attitudes and behavior, and more parent-community support of the school (Taylor & Dorsey-Gaines, 1989; U. S. Census Bureau, 1988; Yao, 1988).

But while parents, teachers, and administrators together strongly favor parental involvement in the schools, and although it seems logical that parental involvement should take place, this is not always the case, especially with African-American, Asian, and Hispanic-American populations. The school's attitude toward the home and community has evolved from an exclusionist philosophy prevalent in the early years of our country's growth. Today, there is much discussion about a partnership among the family/home, the community, and the school. And, as parents become more active and vocal in the educational community, and by nurturing the parents' caring capacity, this partnership may serve to increase the cooperative relationship between family/home and the school. This augers well for society and may very well become a vital tool in the fight for meaningful educational change (First, 1988; Graubard, 1990; Ladson, 1991; Nedler & McFee, 1979).

In consideration of these issues, this book has been organized to provide an analysis of the real meaning of parental involvement in education. Chapter 1 discusses broad emerging change factors as the United States undergoes a transition with resultant modification in family patterns. This chapter gives an overview of the concept of the family: traditional and new roles, and the family as a social network. It presents a general description of what society expects the family to do in terms of child rearing and socialization. Chapter 2 takes a keen look at family patterns and the relationship to the African-American experience in the context of changing socio-economic conditions that affect educational success. It attempts to flesh out, from a set of difficult circumstances, "strands of success" which may be perceived as being worthy of modelling and celebration. Chapter 3 discusses the status of Hispanics in United States—their unique family characteristics as well as recommendations for more Hispanic parental involvement. Chapter 4 describes the ethnic composition of Asians in United States and their unique perceptions of educational excellence. It defines what

Introduction   xi

parental involvement really means for the Asian family. These three chapters look at characteristics associated with ideal parenting, a critical function which includes family members working together, talking things out, and sharing in deliberations regarding success and failure, all within the context of enduring hope, with pride, determination, and persistence being exercised toward a better educational as well as economic future.

Chapter 5 provides information on goals, and on activities and leadership roles of citizens/parents groups that have been formed to provide guidance, monitoring, and leadership in schools. Among the communities discussed here are boards of education, parents' associations, and national parents' networks. Chapter 6 analyzes the different roles parents need to play in advocating for children and communities and in committing themselves to transforming their societies by taking seriously such notions as equality, justice, and freedom. Chapter 7 presents the hypothesis that parents as well as students need to have a positive self-image. This positive self-concept can be achieved when parents and children work together for academic achievement and readiness for school.

A discussion of the specific characteristics of a successful school follows in Chapter 8. These criteria are cogent and encompassing. They include such factors as school climate, leadership, instruction, the thrust for respect, achievement, and excellence, as well as other generic qualities approximating "good" organizational functions.

Chapter 9 presents characteristics of successful students with an emphasis on ability, effort, and parental involvement. This chapter engages the very critical issue of self-concept, which is often at the heart of many problems in the serious business of teaching and learning. How can one, for example, reach, and thereby motivate, individual students who do not believe in themselves and in their own human possibilities, who lack the ability to function as fellow students among peers in terms of strength of character, purpose, and the very will to do so?

Chapter 10, a pivotal point on which the book turns, addresses parents as educators: the first, and often enduring, teachers of children. It discusses the demand for parents to be involved now, more than ever, in schools; parents are to be perceived not as mere visitors to the institution, or as helpmates for cake sales, but rather as viable partners in a teaching-learning transaction where they function in reciprocal relationships, providing counsel and support, helping, and generally serving the school's function in a variety of ways.

Chapter 11 presents recommendations for national and local organizations and agencies, as well as for parents, to improve parental involvement. Chapter 12 lists organizations and agencies (mostly national) that have been recognized as advocates for parents.

This book is for those interested in the cause of parents, those who are perceived as partners in the serious responsibility of educating children and youth and as celebrants in what ought to be a joyous function of teaching and learning, socializing the young, and thereby, assisting in the critical translation of the social heritage.

REFERENCES

Burke, F. G. (1990). *Public education: Who's in charge?* New York: Praeger.

Chavkin, N. F. (1989). A multicultural perspective on parent involvement: Implications on policy and practice. *Education, 109*, 276–285.

Dulney, K. H. (1987). A comprehensive approach for parents: Community involvement. *Illinois School Journal, 67*, 42–48.

First, J. M. (1988). Immigrant children in United States public schools: Challenges with solutions. *Phi Delta Kappan, 70(3)*, 203–210.

Graubard, S. R. (Sept. 7, 1990). Education, race, and ethnicity: Do we understand the factors affecting differential school success among minorities? *New York Teacher,* 16.

Ladson, G. (Spring, 1991). Beyond multicultural illiteracy. *Journal of Negro Education, 60(2),* 147–157.

Nedler, S. E. & McFee, O. D. (1979). *Working with parents.* Belmont, California: Wadsworth Publishing Co.

Taylor, D. & Dorsey-Gaines, C. (1989). *Growing up literate: Learning from inner-city families.* Portsmouth, New Hampshire: Heinemann.

United States Bureau of the Census. (1988). *The Hispanic population in the United States: Advanced report.* (Current Population Reports, Series No. 431, p. 20). Washington, D. C.: Government Printing Office.

Yao, L. (1988). Working effectively with Asian immigrant parents. *Phi Delta Kappan, 70(3),* 223–225.

Parents and Schools

Chapter 1

U.S. FAMILIES IN THE CONTEXT OF CHANGE

About a quarter of a century ago, traditional families in the United States numbered about 60 percent of the population. Contemporary estimates suggest that this count is down to about 7 percent. Over these years, family configurations and life have changed quite dramatically. The dwindling traditional family—characterized as having two parents, one at home, and two (or at most, three) children—is gradually being replaced by a preponderance of two-career couples, single parents, and so-called blended families, with peculiar economic, emotional, social, and interpersonal dynamics which are said to affect parents' decisions about what is considered best for their young children (Apple, 1982; Hirsch, 1987).

In addition to these dramatic changes, the rapid growth of new technologies and the transformation from an industrial to a service-based, information-processing, highly technological, post-industrial society make the critical issue of choices even more difficult. The rate, extent, and complexity of social change now call into question traditional values, ethics, and morality, not only regarding sex, age, race, ethnicity, color, marriage, and gender, but also regarding children and schooling, as well as the concomitant teaching-learning transaction.

CHANGE AND ITS EFFECTS ON TRADITIONAL FAMILIES

The effects of change on traditional families are well defined and pervasive. In particular, divorce and the demise of the extended family configurations, as well as the rapid entry of women into the labor force, have changed the U.S. family in the last three decades. For example, grandparents, once a part of the family constellation, are no longer as available as before to assist with the caring of grandchildren. Also, divorce, once culturally taboo, now shatters a significant percentage of U.S. marriages, leaving millions of children in single-parent families. Women now compose an extensive share of the workforce. In fact, about 70 percent of mothers with school-age children now work (U.S. Department of Health and Human Services, 1990). These factors have radically altered the manner in which traditional families now function.

It is generally believed that the average family—once vibrant, robust, and full of life—has dwindled as education, recreation, and spiritual and value training all take place outside of the home, with schools and other related institutions shouldering much of the responsibility for delivering the socialization services. Working parents who are especially dependent on outside resources are often forced to hire nonfamily members to provide child care or to leave their children at home partially attended to or alone, in order to provide for themselves. Moreover, since child care is expensive and not always readily available, many parents opt for self-care, resulting in a relatively high percentage of elementary and junior high school students being left on their own before and sometimes long after school hours (Center for Population Options, 1990; Hofferth & Hayes, 1989).

This new population of students, often referred to as "latchkey" children, is now defined as being at risk because they are physically and psychologically, as well as academically, vulnerable (Edelman, 1978; Pai, 1990; Perkins, 1986). In their homes, alone and unsupervised for several hours, they suffer from boredom and loneliness. All too often, they miss school which, consequently, has a negative effect on their academic performance and achievement (Chan & Reudan, 1979; Neiser, 1986; Ogbu, 1985; Rothenberg, 1988; Welsh, 1987; Williams, 1990).

Parents who are compelled to work find themselves in the awkward position of having to talk themselves out of their guilt for having diverted time and energy from their families. The fact is, the social dynamics of contemporary life are pushing many parents, albeit with the best intentions, into making many unusual decisions concerning their children. Thus, some parents respond to social pressures while others feel the burdens of financial obligations; still others struggle with the guilt they feel in having chosen between career and family. Of course, there are parents who also deal with some combination of these several pressure points in their lives. Still many more parents share them all.

Of necessity, therefore, a major concern of school people must be to identify parents who need help and to give them the information, support, and permission they need to make healthy educational decisions concerning their children and to help them assume responsibility for sharing in the education of their children. In other words, the family must be assisted in becoming a viable participant in the education of children. This is a necessity whose time has come.

THE FAMILY NETWORK

The family is a fundamental and durable institution; it often provides a bastion, a kind of common sustenance for a whole culture, the various parts of which may differ substantially in other respects. Interaction among members of families may involve encoded customs that reflect a vast range of educational encounters or experiences within and outside a family and are subsequently passed on by socialization from one generation to another.

The family is a configuration in which almost the entire range of human experiences may occur. These experiences may include love, violence, tenderness, honesty, deceit, sharing, power manipulation, informed consent, formal status hierarchy, and decision making. Also within this setting, there may be a variety of educational experiences or encounters, ranging from conscious, systematic instruction to repetitive moment-to-moment influences. These educational encounters or experiences extend through a rich variety of intra-family connections, such as the education of children by parents, of parents by children, of parents by parents, and of siblings by siblings. There is also the interaction between and among all of them. These complex encounters are further compounded by societal factors, such as role differentiation, rights of parents in their participation in educational programs, and their attendant decision-making processes (Behn & Vaupel, 1982; Haley, 1985; London, 1990).

Despite these complexities, it is recognized that the family has a significant impact on the outcome of a child's education and that this impact is often supplemented by a wide variety of intervention programs, resources, and activities which integrate the modification of education within the home and those transactions that supplement a child's education outside the home. Moreover, providing assistance to parents helps them to upgrade their parenting or helping skills, and these skills can serve as part of an educational support system. Hence, the concept of "enculturation," which is used to refer to the process by which a child learns a particular culture, is closely related to the concept of education and embraces much that might also be perceived as teaching and learning, although in this context, what is taught may not always be what is desired and what is taught is not always what is learned.

U.S. Families in the Context of Change

The perception of the family as educator must assume taking into full account the continuous process of change and development within the family, for both adults and children. Here, education is viewed not only as a constant reorganizing and reconstructing of experiences, but also as the conscious teaching of any sort, whether speech, manners, morals, or skills. However perceived, education requires the process of socialization as it occurs in all literate societies in which children learn to restrain their impulses, postpone immediate gratification, walk, talk, and participate in social life. Thus, education is also viewed as the process by which children learn a particular culture (Angus & Jhally, 1989; Asante, 1980; Bloom, 1987; Hirsch, 1987; Ogbu, 1985; Pai, 1990).

There is a wide range of activities in which education takes place within the family. This range may be seen in the interaction between and among members (e.g., husbands, wives, siblings, grandparents, and other relatives and friends). These participants function, directly and indirectly, in the unique process of shared encounters or experiences sometimes referred to as cultural transmission across generations; as political socialization or the enculturation of the individual within the family function; and as development, teaching, and learning in a different setting. Implicit in these experiences or encounters is the carry-through of systematic, sustained, and deliberate efforts to transmit, evoke, share, and acquire knowledge, attitudes, values, skills, and sensibilities, as well as the learning that results from the efforts, directly or indirectly, intended or unintended. A key concern is the inclusion of a deliberate process or a set of processes that is at the margins of awareness, and which must be brought forward in a variety of settings.

Within the context of the dynamics of change across the United States, families will in all likelihood continue very much in their traditional evolutionary trends. The foreseeable future will, doubtless, continue to be characterized by differing structures and life styles, legacies of freedom of choice, even as the nation struggles to maintain a cultural norm of the nuclear family unit.

Concomitantly, adjustments will have to be made, not only to accommodate these changing configurations, which cultural sanctions have accepted as part of the nation's mores, but also to accommodate the telling educational demands—for example, the growing awareness of diversity in cognitive styles. It is in part because of these considerations that schools will be required to play their vital roles as key instruments of the socializing process, mechanisms, or institutions bearing the awesome responsibilities for transmitting the civilizing mission of rights and responsibilities, vital aspects of the cultural heritage.

How these goals get accomplished will be a national challenge of the future. It is a challenge that will require the complement of all the various publics, agencies, institutions, groups, and individuals, including parents, who must participate significantly in the dynamic responsibility of cultivating the nation's most important resource, its children and youth, the next generation of U.S. citizens.

It is possible to accomplish such a task. It can, and indeed must, be done. A first step on this protracted journey must now begin with the significant inclusion of parents in serious and realistic societal and educational decision making. It has already been shown that parents can and do contribute positively to children's early intellectual development. When parents are involved, schools are helped, student's self-esteem and achievement are improved; also, by working together with school people, parents are helped to improve their own self-worth while acquiring useful skills. The interaction is reciprocal. In fact, when parents are involved, communication between parents and teachers improves and schools become better places for everyone, since all participants work toward a common goal, the education of the student.

In addition, when parents are involved, the home and community, and thus the school, benefit. Participatory democracy is at work and the value-added effect is a more informed polity. It is also a polity of shared responsibility which strives for educational health through a dynamic home-school-community partnership. Moreover, parents and parent-surrogates (i.e., teachers who are informed about the processes of early childhood development and who are nurturing and caring toward young children) can be effectively trained and encouraged by culturally sensitive and informed advocates of children to promote the well-being of youngsters (Campbell, 1991; Herber et al., 1972; Slaughter, 1983).

The input of parents in the educative process is, now more than ever, of paramount urgency. In accepting parents as their children's first teachers, it would seem a cogent move to extend their vital participation toward the formal education of their own children, by first removing the barriers to their entry, and by then providing them with the fullest support in terms of principles, methods, procedures, goods, and services.

The efficaciousness of such involvement must go well beyond the immediacy of the child and its family to the larger society. A healthy society must strive collectively to secure its future by seeing that its youth have the skills to appreciate and live the good life. This implies having an understanding of the accumulated wisdom of the family as to what constitutes a good life. Here, the assumption is that with hard work and a little luck, parents can give their children a better and more abundant life than they have had. This act is implicit in the notion of the acculturation and transmission of the cultural legacy, which schools and other related institutions must work collaboratively to promulgate.

For many people the concept of the good life still prevails; but for many, too, there is an accompanying and uneasy sense that something has gone radically awry. This concern, this disquiet, includes the neglect of the nation's most potent natural resource, our children, and those primarily engaged in their care, their parents, who must be brought into the serious engagement in the teaching-learning transaction of their children.

But, more than this, contemporary decision makers must see their future educational responsibilities in relation to the past, which is different. Today's youth must be helped to see their strengths, recognize their potential, develop their abilities, and accept their responsibilities under altered social circumstances in a changing world, in which families continue to be the basic social units of every culture.

REFERENCES

Angus, I. & Jhally, S. (Eds.). (1989). *Cultural politics in contemporary America.* New York: Routledge.

Apple, M. (1982). *Education and power.* New York: Routledge.

Asante, M. K. (1980). *Afrocentricity: The theory of social change.* Buffalo, New York: Amulefi.

Behn, R. D. & Vaupel, R. D. (1982). *Quick analysis for busy decision makers.* New York: Basic Books.

Bloom, A. (1987). *The closing of the American mind.* New York: Simon and Schuster.

Campbell, F. (1991). The Carolina Abecedarian Project: Age 12 Follow-up. Paper presented at the biennial meeting of the Society for Research in Child Development, Seattle, Washington.

Center for Population Options. (1990). *Adolescent sexuality, pregnancy and parenthood.* Washington, D. C.: Center for Population Options.

Chan, K. S. & Reudan, R. (1979). Poverty and culture in education: Separate but equal. *Journal of the Council for Exceptional Children, 45,* 422–428.

Edelman, M. W. (1978). *Families in peril: An agenda for social change.* Cambridge, Massachusetts: Harvard University Press.

Haley, B. (1985). *This way to school success: In the report card trap.* White Hall, Virginia: Betterway Publications.

Herber, R., Garber, H., Harrington, S. & Hoffman, C. (1972). Rehabilitation of families for mental retardation. (Progress Report). Washington, D. C.: U.S. Department of Health, Education, and Welfare.

Hirsch, E. D. (1987). *Cultural literacy.* Boston: Houghton Mifflin.

Hofferth, S. L. & Hayes, C. D. (Eds.). (1989). *Risking the future: Adolescent sexuality, pregnancy, and childbearing.* (Volume 2: Working Papers and statistical reports). Washington, D. C.: National Academy Press.

London, C. B. G. (January, 1990). Parental empowerment: Going beyond chalk and talk. *Black Issues in Higher Education, 6*(21), 136.

Neiser, U. (1986). *The school achievement of minority children: New perspectives.* Hillsdale, New Jersey: Earlbaum.

Ogbu, L. U. (1985). Research currents: Cultural ecological influences on minority school learning. *Language Arts, 62*(8), 860–869.

Pai, Y. (1990). *Cultural foundations of education.* Columbus, Ohio: Merrill.

Perkins, U. E. (1986). *Harvesting new generations: The positive development of black youth.* Chicago: Third World Press.

Rothenberg, P. (1988). Integrating the study of race, gender, and class: Some preliminary observations. *Feminist Teacher, 3*(3), 37–42.

Slaughter, D. (1983). Early intervention and its effect on maternal and child development. Monographs of the Society for Research in Child Development, Series No. 202, 48(4).

United States Department of Health and Human Services. (1990). *Monthly Vital Statistics Report, 39*(4).

Welsh, C. E. (1987). Schooling and the civic exclusion of Latinos: Toward a discourse of dissonance. *Journal of Education, 169*(2), 115–131.

Williams, L. (May, 1990). *In looks, a sense of racial unity. New York Times,* pp. 1, 8.

Chapter 2

THE AFRICAN-AMERICAN EXPERIENCE IN FAMILY CONTEXT

The designation "African American" is used in this book as a generic term that defines and includes several ethnic groups of people who have derived their genealogical essence from the African continent and who have come to the United States through circumstances of chance or choice (Banks, 1981; Levy & Renaldo, 1975; Sowell, 1978). Therefore, reference to these groups implies that they came from Africa directly, or indirectly by way of such areas as the Caribbean, Latin America, or wherever else people of African descent have lived over time (Feris, 1913; Herskovits, 1958; Keto, 1990; Nobles, 1986; Ravitch, 1990 & 1990; Richards, 1991; Sudarkasa, 1981; Van Sertima, 1976).

These ethnic groups of people of African descent are hereinafter referred to as the African Diaspora or the Black Diaspora. It must also be noted that apart from the many native languages spoken throughout continental Africa, there is to be considered the fact that through the force of dominance which has grown out of conquest, slavery, and/or colonization, many languages and dialects have been added to the already established repertoire of communication mechanisms, often allowing many persons within these groups to become multilingual (Bickerton, 1975; Cohen, Fraenkel & Brewer, 1968; Craig, 1978; Haskins & Butler, 1973; Sudarkasa, 1981; Valdman, 1977). These basic issues of consideration are only a part of the varying characteristics of African Americans, members of the African Diaspora, the largest ethnic group in the United States, whose history did not begin with slavery and who are referred to hereinafter as Black Americans or African Americans (Hale-Benson, 1988).

AFRICENTRIC PEOPLE IN THE UNITED STATES

In the United States, the heinous institution of slavery systematically rendered most African Americans monolingual. The severe restrictions on the use of native languages as means of communication and, more critically, on the use of the drum have destroyed whatever vestiges of languages enslaved Africans brought with them. Here and there, in pockets of isolation, such as the Sea Islands, as well as in other areas that are coterminous to the Carolinas, the Virginias, Maryland, and Florida, remnants of African languages (e.g., the Gullah language) survive with much modification, including peculiar permutations (Feris, 1913; Froebenius, 1913; Johnson, 1910; Marquet, 1972; Nobles, 1974; Rogers, 1961).

In the Caribbean, for example, where there was also slavery and still are aspects of colonialism, people of African descent speak English, French, Dutch, and Spanish, as well as attendant variations, including pidgins and Creoles, which are derivatives of these languages (Diop, 1974; Hymes, 1971; James, 1976). And, although some persons in the United States may not readily admit to a personal or individual ethnic identification, still many do. For people of African descent, especially those who hail directly from countries in Africa, the Caribbean, and the Americas, ethnicity is tied to physical characteristics, such as skin color. Major decisions affecting such persons are usually predicated on those characteristics in the United States, where, for example, immigration criteria include major phenotypical considerations.

Ethnic groups in the African Diaspora share many commonalities. Of primary importance is the visibility of color and other physical characteristics. But although the characteristic of color unifies people of African ancestry, marked cultural differences exist to distinguish among the various ethnic groups. Nonetheless, it is not uncommon for decision makers to lump all Africentric ethnic groups together. It is also known that much misunderstanding and many erroneous assumptions often undergird decisions which ultimately affect the form and function of educational goods and services that are designed for such groups. Moreover, emanating from the tragedy of slavery is the notion that most of the ethnic groups of Africentric antecedents defy the frequently touted goal of assimilation, a traditional U.S. ethic which has so far remained largely a Eurocentric possibility at best and minimally achieved at worst. In fact, the assumption of the Melting Pot Theory has remained essentially a dream, since people continue to associate within their own particular ethnic group to a degree that gives rise to the idea of a "salad-bowl" notion in which the vegetables are joined by the tenuous relationship of the mayonnaise as the only holding element.

From the standpoint of educational decision making, it is imperative that school people heighten their awareness of students' unique cultural characteristics and other social nuances, such as their life and cognitive styles, that are specific to the various Africentric ethnic groups. Moreover, of necessity, there is the need to recognize that while there are many cultural universals, such as similarities of human, moral, and educational dimensions, there are also marked differences that are special to these groups. But, more importantly, it is false to assume that such differences imply deficiencies. On the contrary, these differences should be seen as possible factors of magnificent educational interest to be understood and celebrated; that likewise, these factors should serve to enrich the unique pluralistic population and cultures of the United States. They all enrich the nation, making it unique among others.

To understand how these special characteristics may give rise to certain assumptions requires some pertinent explanations about history, including African-American history, the African-American presence in the United States, and the effects of that presence on African-American families.

THE UNITED STATES AND AFRICAN-AMERICAN HISTORY

Although African Americans make up the largest ethnic group in the United States today and have made and continue to make significant contributions to business, education, entertainment, medicine, politics, the arts, religion, and virtually every other field of endeavor, U.S. history in general is almost devoid of African-American history. In fact, traditional U.S. history, following a strategy of exclusion, has long relegated African Americans to near invisibility. Even when contemporary scholars undertake the task of restoring the missing balance, they are often criticized as being revisionists (DePalmer, 1990; Douglas, 1991; Gardner, 1990; London, 1989; Ravitch, 1990; Sobol, 1990; Wiley, 1990). Notwithstanding such accusations, the truth remains that African-American history is central to U.S. history. Of paramount importance is placing in proper perspective the significance of African-American history. Traditional history has portrayed the peopling of the United States by Spanish *conquistadores*, French trappers, and the arrival of Captain John T. Smith and the Pilgrims, with their descendants pouring through the gaps in the Appalachians and making their way in covered wagons to the other shining sea, the Pacific Ocean.

In fact, for every white immigrant to the Western Hemisphere, four or five blacks were brought as enslaved persons. Not until the middle of the 19th century did white immigration exceed black presence, meaning that the hemisphere until that time was an extension of Africa, rather than of Europe (Levy & Renaldo, 1975; Sowell, 1981). In addition, more of these blacks participated in the dynamics of the labor market, working longer hours and producing what was more valuable than free labor was able or willing to do. Interestingly, and of great economic import, the organization of society in England and Western Europe, based on a landed aristocracy and a free labor force, was never duplicated in the United States, the Caribbean, or Latin America. The British colonies in the North had no landed aristocracy and, without slaves, there was none in the South or the Caribbean.

The farmers of British colonial United States were duly motivated to do more than subsist and produce profitable export crops. Therefore, the foreign earnings of British colonial United States resulted overwhelmingly from the labor of plantation slaves. Thus, in the generation preceding the American Revolution, increasing numbers of slaves were dragged out of Africa, plantation crops poured out of the colonies, and with the earnings of these crops and the sale of slaves, colonial merchants and planters, fishermen, and farmers increasingly enjoyed imported British goods.

African Americans have functioned in a variety of capacities that indeed transcend the basic agricultural pursuits of slavery. And yet, traditional U.S. history has neglected the role of blacks in the growth and development of this country. The study of the African-American family must begin with the study of African-American history in order to remove myths and to provide a truer understanding of history and its impact on black families whose children are part of the kaleidoscopic landscape of the U.S. population.

Quite apart from the exclusion of African-American history with its component of the heinous slave experience and its consequences, many persons just simply refuse to acknowledge that blacks in the United States and the Americas, as well as the Caribbean, share some common core historical experiences and cultural patterns that continue to shape present-day life styles. Still others apparently forget or choose to forget that in spite of overwhelming barriers and long-standing discriminatory practices, African Americans who were brought as enslaved persons from Africa had already experienced a rich history of social, cultural, economic, and political development, which began long before many of the civilizations of Western Europe.

Indeed, blacks have contributed to all phases of U.S. growth and development. Simultaneously, they have shaped and reshaped the heritage of their African origins as well as their peculiar American experiences into distinctive life styles in the years between 1619 (when the first enslaved persons were brought to the United States) and the present. Blacks, on leaving Africa, carried the memory and imprint of their heritage across successive generations in their songs, socialization processes, social behaviors, institutions, and value systems. Since their arrival in the New World, blacks have developed a wide range of alternative functional institutions and life styles. But, dulled by the unfulfilled promises of the "American dream," such equally compelling yet conflicting impulses have forced many blacks to fashion for themselves something of a dual identity as U.S. citizens and as African Americans. These impulses have also led to the creation of value systems, behavioral patterns, and institutional structures that affirm and validate their own humanity. They also provide a means of survival in the larger society which is often perceived to be hostile to blacks.

Thus, although different operational details and behavioral variations exist among African Americans, they do not invalidate the existence of a unanimity of basic cultural components, which grew out of an essential core of consensus based on shared experiences (Kellogg, 1988; London, 1990; Muller & Espenshad, 1985; Sowell, 1981). Cultural parallels may be observed among blacks in the United States, the Caribbean, and Central and South America. The extent of

African retentions in contemporary African-American life styles and the variations in degrees of acculturation and assimilation among blacks in the United States all attest to the fact that it is indeed imperative that the public, particularly school people, become aware of these historical factors in order to understand the circumstances (i.e., the immigration and adjustment of blacks to the U.S. conditions, their cultural modifications, and the felt presence of African history and culture) and in order to understand African-American family structures and the links associated with their children who attend U.S. schools.

Today, black families must be understood from a perspective that recognizes the cultural variations, functionality, and validity of black family life styles. For example, most black parents, as do most parents of every society, socialize their children to become self-sufficient, competent adults as defined by the society in which they live. For African-American families, living in the United States has always meant that socialization occurs within the ambiguities of a cultural heritage that is both African and European American, as well as with the influences of a social system that abstractly espouses both democratic equality for all citizens and caste-like status for its black citizens.

That indeed is the reality of the African American in general. Thus, although mainstream social scientists have, in general, appreciated the uniqueness of blacks, research on black families and their children has usually been simplistic and often pejorative in approach (McAdoo, 1981). The truth is, however, that black children are socialized to grow and develop to become self-sufficient, competent adults in the face of real constraints U.S. society places on African Americans.

The lives of African-American parents and their child-rearing approaches are embedded in the social, political, and economic situations of the culture. In this sense, the behaviors and life styles of African Americans are different from those of European Americans. Child-rearing priorities, attitudes, and patterns of behaviors have developed out of the exigencies of the unique economic, cultural, and racial circumstances in which they live every day. These cultural styles and child-rearing approaches, unique to black families, have enabled them to provide supportive and effective environments for the development of African-American children. The strict, no-nonsense discipline of black parents, often characterized as "harsh" or "rigid" by mainstream-oriented observers, remains part of the family institution of socialization and has been shown to be functional, appropriate discipline of caring parents. Similarly, the emphasis on obedience is very positively grounded and of special significance to parents who view this demand as implying respect, love, and a significant aspect of preparation for the serious business of life, of achieving in school, and thus "making it" in the harsh realities of the world.

THE AFRICAN-AMERICAN FAMILY: IMPEDIMENTS AND PROGRESS

From the inception of enslavement, African Americans have been plagued by the dynamics of impediments that grow out of the insidious institution of racism. Racism in the United States has always been primarily an affair in black and white. Although other minorities, such as Indians, Asians, and Hispanics, have been subjected to measures of racial degradation and exploitation, in this nation the dominant institutional forms of racism have essentially focused on persons of African ancestry. The massive reliance on police power to control black communities, particularly in the cities, is striking evidence of this underlying conflict (Knowles & Prewitt, 1969, pp. 137–138).

The ideology of racism has been a major feature of the U.S. tradition, at least since the 18th century. It has been so well established that it now has a life of its own, and is clearly reflective of the social conditions it rationalizes (Knowles &

Prewitt, 1969) or attempts to ignore. In this context, blacks have been historically relegated to the bottom of the status ladder. Slavery defined a class to which only persons of African ancestry belonged. With the abolition of slavery, rural tenant farming, or the peonage system, became the bottom status and it has been shared with poor whites in a minimal way. But, even though class distinction did begin to develop within the black community with the growth of a small professional class and a smaller business class, the overall, national class structure, even in modern urban settings, is very much a truncated one.

Today, despite small gains, blacks are still virtually excluded from corporate proprietorships and management, which are the major determinants of high and controlling status in U.S. society. By and large, blacks do not even have the kinds of ownership, occupations, incomes, or education that confer the least of the advantageous social ranks. And, moreover, since blacks are more concentrated at the lower status levels than whites are, the present hierarchial class structure operates, in addition to race, as a means of reinforcing the subordinate positions of blacks (Knowles & Prewitt, 1969; pp. 164–165). These conditions are evident throughout the nation.

In essence, the racial distinctions created in any one institutional area operate as instruments supporting the segregation and unequal treatment taking place in other institutions. In other words, there is a synergistic as well as a symbiotic relationship between and among the institutions. The school systems, for example, use the neighborhood policy, which, combined with residential segregation, operates as a surrogate for direct segregation. Suburbs, by creating very restrictive zoning regulations or urban renewal developments that set universally high rents, can eliminate all but the very few black families on the basis of income. Therefore, given the racial differentials produced by a school system, an employer, by using its regular personnel tests and criteria, can screen out most blacks from desirable jobs. Thus, knowledge of the links between the circumstances of the larger ecological environment and their implications for children at school should raise one's understanding of the "societal baggage" carried along and of the impediments such baggage creates for the teaching-learning transaction even in the best schools.

The family is the most important social unit in any society (Williams, 1990). A healthy family experience is important for one to develop and maintain social and mental health. Being part of a family gives one a sense of belonging and provides members with a bond that is sealed by common blood. Any system that deprives a people of its family structure denies the humanity of that people. Slavery focused on destroying the positive self-images of blacks by destroying the black family structure. The black family has not completely recovered from the fallout of slavery because many factors and behaviors that derive from the experiences of slavery continue today. Black families in the African Diaspora have had to struggle against all odds to triumph over numerous impediments—physical, mental, psychological, spiritual, social, and cultural—as well as to grow and succeed (Williams, 1990).

Notwithstanding these imponderables, the diversity of black families, their value systems, and life styles point to a difficulty of addressing the families of African Americans. For one thing, within the field of black families are such designations as Black, African American, Afro-American, and Negro (McAdoo, 1981). In the black community, the notion of the family lies in the attempt to survive economically, develop relationships in order to procreate, and raise children and move as advocates for their children and families.

By drawing upon the cultural relativistic view, it is to be understood that the black family, despite all the impediments of racism, has remained a functional entity. Since the United States is a plural society, differences are largely accounted for by the variation in cultural backgrounds and the many problems that emanate from the decline of old forms of traditional, extended, and nuclear families. Emerging configurations are surfacing alongside some enduring traditional modalities, such as those of African-American families.

In talking about family successes, parenting, and working together, African-American strengths are reflected in the general ability to provide the necessary functions to members and nonmembers in a basic, viable family unit. Such provisions include the operational support of the ability of the family to meet the needs of its members and the demands made upon it by systems and institutions outside of the immediate family units. Otto (1962), in an examination of this phenomenon, identified family strengths of African Americans as showing:

1. A concern for family unity, loyalty, and inter-family cooperation;
2. An ability for self-help and to accept help when appropriate;
3. An ability to perform family roles flexibly;
4. An ability to establish and maintain growth-producing relationships within and without the family; and
5. The ability to provide for the physical, emotional, and spiritual needs of the family (pp. 72–82).

In addition to some general, functional characteristics which have undergirded African-American families, in terms of survival, development, and stability, there are also strong kinship bonds, strong work orientation, the adaptability of family roles, strong achievement drives and orientation, and a sense of strong religious orientation (Hill, 1972, p. 172). These survival skills and roles link the various groups together.

In the United States, the consideration of these characteristics in the context of African-American experiences reflects life styles which, despite economic and social impediments, sharply define this constituency of citizens. There are strong kinship ties which, for example, bind members into taking additional relatives into their households. This unique absorption of individuals includes minors as well as the elderly. In addition, informal adoption is another characteristic that defines African Americans. It involves acceptance of community members as members of existing family units, with full rights and responsibilities. It is primarily an ancient custom of African family incorporation. Indeed, this mixture of family ties generates and maintains the extended family in which members share. It also serves to lengthen the support of intra-family ties, as well as those between the institutions of the school and home. It also suggests and fosters cooperation, support networks, and the act of working and sharing together in a spirit of "communitas." Thus, when educationally oriented deficiencies emerge, it is almost guaranteed that group efforts will be consistently utilized to enhance students' life spaces and attitudes to education, teaching, and learning.

Unfortunately, many issues surrounding the education of African-American children have been discussed against a backdrop of misguided mental sets (McLaren, 1986; McLaren & Dantley, 1990; Yeakey & Bennett, 1990). Mental sets are preset impressions harbored and cultivated in the minds of individuals, which govern and sometimes control the ability for proaction and reaction. Mental sets are harmful, even when they favor African Americans, Hispanics, Asians, or other minorities. Mindsets are based on preconceived notions which are often grounded in stereotypes. An example is the assumption that many African-American children, in the context of being students, need a mother, a father, sister, or brother image more than they need academics (McLaren, 1986; McLaren & Dantley, 1990; Yeakey, 1991; Yeakey & Bennett, 1990). Substituting these images for the teaching of subject-matter content has all too frequently defeated the otherwise possibly good intentions of many teachers. This point is not meant to imply that the development of good, personal relationships with students should be discouraged. Far from it! It is to say, however, that all too often, many teachers, in both the private and public sectors, spend an inordinate amount of time on image substitution, rather than on academics, in the classroom. By doing so, instead of delivering on their professional responsibilities to teach black students responsibly, they frequently miss the authenticity of their mission of professional responsibility. By taking this stand, one can reason that the import of such action is predicated on the notion that making emotional geniuses and academic paraplegics is more important for African-American students. This attitude has assumed systemic proportions; the "placing" of large numbers of African-American children in special education classes is a case in point. Today, special education of African-American children has become a big educational growth industry in school systems of many large urban areas.

In fact, teachers ought to be teaching the whole child to his or her fullest potential, all of the issues, ideas, and concepts that are requisite for total living. Instead, there is often the pervasive and telling assumption behind which many teachers hide in urban schools, as they articulate the negative view that African-American parents and children are not concerned about education (Cooley, 1964; Denzin, 1970). This assumption is absurd, groundless, and smacks of irresponsibility. Such deep-rooted stereotypes and myths hide a determined refusal to face the real issues, which include meeting students' needs by teaching them properly, instead of indulging in the luxury of blaming the victims of an otherwise insensitive and, in many ways, oppressive school system.

African-American families, despite overwhelmingly negative social and economic circumstances that often plague their lives, have been bulwarks of achievement, often proving to be flexible and adaptable instruments for both their survival and advancement, providers of critical nurturance missing in the African-American experience (Billingsley, 1968; Carter, 1986; Deutsch, 1991). They just do not give up in the face of adversity; instead, they seek multiple ways of improving themselves against all of the apparent odds.

Education is one of the main avenues by which African Americans are able to lift themselves from society's ascribed low status. Hence, it is imperative that African Americans maintain heightened interest in the attainment of a sound education for their children. Blacks know this better than anyone else, including those who assume to talk on their behalf. But, by and large, much resistance is found in the way of progress. Making substantive economic and educational advancement remains a persistent struggle for African Americans. They continue their historical struggle, which began with enslavement, against all odds, to achieve what other U.S. citizens often take for granted. For African Americans, quality education remains a sure passport to freedom of participation in the polity (Patterson, 1972; Valentine, 1968).

It has been mentioned earlier in this chapter that the issue of language has become a critical factor for ethnic groups within the African Diaspora. African-American children who come to schools from a distinct or basically African-rooted culture are often given the burden of adapting to the U.S. mainstream culture, which is, by definition, a second culture. Most European Americans do not face this difficulty, for theirs is the mainstream culture; and yet blacks are always measured against European Americans in every educational assessment.

One outgrowth of this conflict or difficulty of norming blacks against European Americans has prompted research in this area. Currently, a group of psychologists and educators is investigating perceived distinctions between black and white children's learning styles (Hale-Benson, 1988). By using the impact of culture, including language, economics, geography, personality, and performance differences, the immediate discourse has placed theorists into two camps: one emphasizing the group, the other focusing on the individual African-American child (Berger, 1988). Berger reports that there are distinctive learning styles among African-American children. However, upon entering school, blacks are expected to have already mastered white, mainstream cultural concepts and objectives.

Berger (1988) further argues that language is generally used differently among black members than it is by white members of the U.S. society. Moreover, while black children may be better at generating ideas orally than writing them down, decision makers usually draw inferences about the children's ability from their writing. Issues of relationship, family size, and the socialization processes are juxtaposed with the teaching-learning transaction, the question of teacher sensitivity, warmth, and encouragement as conditions that teachers use for gaining higher achievement among black children. Eschewing the notion of lumping black children together, Strickland is reported by Berger (1988) to have argued that good teaching is the key ingredient. She refers to the wide variations among African-American children, based on economic, geographical, and personality differences.

In light of these factors, it is reasoned that assigning attributes to children in terms of ethnic background ignores the individual capacities. Placing the emphasis on good teaching for all children, black and white, still remains, it would seem, the most viable principle. Success for all children must become the mandate of education. To teach all children to the zenith of their capacities ought to become the preoccupation of educational decision makers, with teachers effectuating this commitment through action in the classrooms. The problem goes far beyond implicit or explicit effort to stultify the inclusion of African Americans as democratic participants in the life of the nation, the legacies of slavery and racism notwithstanding.

LOOKING TO THE FUTURE

A primary requirement for the facilitation of the teaching-learning transaction is the teacher-student classroom interaction. Teachers' knowledge of their students and how they relate to such students are very crucial issues for teaching and learning. Good interaction in a classroom as well as at the "teaching home" enhances the joy of teaching and nurtures the educative process. The removal of obstacles to this process is therefore critical. For African-American students, this need to remove obstacles to educational progress is even more critical, since traditional stereotypical encumbrances have created barriers to teaching and learning, generally.

According to McAdoo (1988), the removal of educational barriers from African-American students must begin with the families. And demythologizing African-American families must aim to go beyond the negative stereotypical views that have been held as the status on black families. These, unfortunately, are views often held by those in positions to make policy and programmatic decisions that have direct impact on the lives of students of black families. The demythologizing of negative images about African-American families must therefore remain an ongoing process for the removal of ethnocentric concepts held by mainstream social science literature, which encourages poor attitudinal behaviors in many classrooms. Among the many myths are the following:

1. That blacks are simply who they are because they are poor; that if poverty was removed, then there would be a congruence of values and structures between and among all families;
2. That poverty and the experiences of slavery and Reconstruction have left an indelible mark on families, and that this mark has persisted to the present; and,
3. That black families are unique because of the remnants of African culture that have been maintained and adapted to discrimination (McAdoo, 1988, pp. 10–11).

In fact, these views are now the subject of investigation by black scholarship, as efforts are being made to clarify the issues and put them in proper perspective. For while one must support the view of those who feel that poverty and discrimination are the major factors impinging on black families, common patterns have been found in non-Western families on the African continent, in the Caribbean, Latin America, and in isolated areas of rural United States, prompting the acknowledgment of some cultural continuities. The circumstances of African-American families include these and more, and students of African-American descent encounter enormous barriers that emanate from these compelling circumstances.

The reality is that the education of black students cannot be explained in isolation from the black family. Black family organization cannot be explained without reference to the social contexts from which it has been derived (Nobles, 1974, 1978). Thus, whereas black families can be analyzed as groups with strategies for coping with wider societal forces (Stack, 1974), they must also be understood as institutions with historical traditions that set them apart, as formations that are not identical to, or pathological variants of, family structures found among other groups in the United States (Sudarkasa, 1981, p. 38).

African families, for example, like those in other parts of the world, embody two contrasting bases for membership: consanguinity, which refers to kinship that is commonly assumed or presumed to be biologically based on and rooted in "blood ties," and affinity, which refers to kinship that is created by law and rooted "in law" (Marshall, 1968). Thus, African families have traditionally been organized around consanguineal cores that are formed by adult siblings of the same sex or by larger same-sex segments of patri- or matrilineages.

For educators interested in the heritage of Europe, Asia, Australia, the Americas, and Africa in African-American family organization, a study of the operation of the principles of conjugality and consanguinity in these families would provide considerable insight into the ways that these two family institutional traditions have been interwoven. By looking at the differential impact of these principles in matters of household formation, delegation of authority, maintenance of solidarity and support, acquisition and transmission of property, and financial management and, by examining the political and economic variables that favor the predominance of one or the other principle, investigators may emerge with questions and formulations that can move general understanding of the issue beyond the debates over "pathology" and "normalcy" in African-American family life. Such efforts are pertinent for understanding African-American families and the cultural nuances that students usually take with them to school and for acknowledging the necessity of incorporating parental input in educational decision making as well as the teaching-learning transaction (Sudarkasa, 1981). In addition to these there are concerns with broader factors, such as what significant others need to know and how this knowledge, taken in the best of faith, can be wisely used to remove doubts and stereotypical assumptions and thus help to facilitate the serious responsibility of educating one of the nation's largest ethnic groups.

Political and economic values are always part of any explanation of family formation and function. The cultural, historical derivation of formation helps to explain the nature of adaptation to peculiar political and economic contexts. Since it is beyond the scope of this chapter to present a holistic explanation of African-American experience in family context, treatment has been restricted to an explanation of how in the face of compelling adversity black family organization and function differ from that of other groups in the United States, and how related factors, derived from these circumstances, are played out at school during the teaching-learning transaction.

REFERENCES

Banks, J. A. (1981). *Multiethnic education*. Boston: Allyn & Bacon.

Berger, J. (July 6, 1988). What do they mean by "Black learning style"? *New York Times Education Section*.

Bickerton, D. (1975). *Dynamics of a Creole system*. Cambridge: Cambridge University Press.

Billingsley, A. (1968). *Black families in white America*. Englewood Cliffs, New Jersey: Prentice-Hall.

Carter, T. (1986). *Shattering illusions*. London: Lawrence & Wishart.

Cohen, R., Fraenkel, G., and Brewer, J. (1968). The language of the hard core poor: Implications for cultural conflict. *Sociology Quarterly, 10*, 19–28.

Cooley, C. H. (1964). *Human nature and the social order*. New York: Shocken. (Originally published in 1902).

Craig, D. R. (1978). The sociology of language learning and teaching in a Creole situation. *Caribbean Journal of Education, 5*(3), 101–116.

Denzin, N. K. (1970). *The research act*. Chicago: AVC.

DePalmer, A. (November, 1990). The culture question. *New York Times Educational Supplement*, pp. 22–30.

Deutsch, C. H. (February, 1991). Coping with cultural polyglots. *New York Times, Business Section*, p. 25.

Diop, C. A. (1974). *African origin of civilization: Myth of reality*. New York: Lawrence Hill.

Douglas, M. (January, 1991). Making a case for multicultural education. *New York City Amsterdam News*, p. 13.

Feris, W. H. (1913). *The African abroad*. 2 vols. New Haven, Connecticut: The Turtle, Morehouse and Taylor Press.

Froebenius, L. (1913). *The voice of Africa*. 2 vols. London: Hutchinson & Co.

Gardner, B. (1990). A crucible for change. *Education Week, 10*(4), 26.

Hale-Benson, J. H. (1988). *Black children: Their roots, culture, and learning styles*. Baltimore: Johns Hopkins University Press.

Haskins, J. & Butler, H. F. (1973). *The psychology of Black language.* New York: Barnes and Noble.

Herskovits, M. J. (1958). *Myths of the Negro past.* Boston: Beacon Press.

Hill, R. B. (1972). *The strengths of black families.* New York: Book Press.

Hymes, D. (1971). *Piginization and creolization of languages.* Cambridge: Cambridge University Press.

James, G. M. (1976). *Stolen legacy.* San Francisco: Julian Richardson.

Johnson, H. H. (1910). *The Negro in the New World.* London: Methuen & Co.

Kellogg, J. B. (1988). Faces of change. *Phi Delta Kappan, 70*(3), 199–204.

Keto, C. T. (1990). *African-centered perspective of history.* Blackwood, New Jersey: C. A. Associates.

Knowles, L. L. & Prewitt, K. (Eds.). (1969). *Institutional racism.* Englewood Cliffs, New Jersey: Prentice-Hall.

Levy, E. & Renaldo, J. (1975). *America's people.* Glenview, Illinois: Scott Foresman & Co.

London, C. B. G. (1990). Educating young new immigrants: How can the United States cope? *International Journal of Adolescence and Youth, 2*(2), 81–100.

———. (1989). Recent immigrant children in American schools: Are they lost? *Journal of New York State Association for Bilingual Education, 5,* 1–19.

Marquet, J. (1972). *Civilization of Black Africa.* London: Oxford University Press.

Marshall, C. A. (Miara Sudarkasa) (1968). Marriage: Comparative analysis. In *International Encyclopedia of the Social Sciences.* Vol. 10. New York: Macmillan/Free Press.

McAdoo, H. P. (Ed.) (1988). *Black families.* Beverly Hills, California: Sage Publications.

McLaren, P. L. (1986). *Schooling as a ritual performance: Toward a political economy of education symbols and gestures*. London and New York: Routledge.

McLaren, P. L. & Dantley, B. (Winter, 1990). Leadership and a critical pedagogy of race: Cornel West, Stuart Hall, and the Prophetic tradition. *Journal of Negro Education, 59*(1), 29–44.

Muller, T. & Espenshad, T. (1985). *The four waves*. Washington, D. C.: Urban Institute Press.

Nobles, W. (June, 1974). Africanity: Its role in Black families. *Black Scholar, 9*, 10–17.

Nobles, W. (1986). *African psychology*. Oakland, California: Black Family Institute.

Nobles, W. (November, 1978). Toward an empirical and theoretical framework for defining Black families. *Journal of Marriage and the Family, 40*, 670–688.

Otto, H. A. (1962). What is a strong family? *Marriage and Family Living, 24*, 72–82.

Patterson, O. (1972). Rethinking Black history. *African Report. 17*, 29–31.

Ravitch, D. (1990). Diversity and democracy. *American Educator, 14*, 16–20.

Ravitch, D. (Summer, 1990). Multiculturalism: E pluribus plures. *American Scholar*, 337–354.

Richards, D. (1991). *Let the circle be unbroken*. Trenton, New Jersey: Africa World Press.

Rogers, J. A. (1961). *Africa's gift to America*. New York: Futuro Press.

Sobol, T. (1990). Understanding diversity. *Educational Leadership, 48*(3), 27–30.

Sowell, T. (1981). *Ethnic America: A history*. New York: Basic Books.

Stack, C. (1974). *All our kin*. New York: Harper and Row.

Sudarkasa, N. (1981). Interpreting the African heritage in Afro-American family organization. In McAdoo, H. P. (Ed.), *Black families* (pp. 37–53). Beverly Hills, California: Sage Publications.

Valdman, A. (1977). *Pidgin and Creole linguistics*. Bloomington, Indiana: Indiana University Press.

Valentine, C. (1968). *Culture and poverty*. Chicago: University of Chicago Press.

Van Sertima, I. (1976). *They came before Columbus*. New York: Random House.

Wiley, D. (1990). How deep is the seated commitment to diversity? *Black Issues in Higher Education, 7*(21), 1, 6–7.

Williams, R. (1990). *They stole it, but you must return it*. Rochester, New York: HEMA Publishing.

Yeakey, C. C. (1991). Schooling: A political analysis of the distribution of power and privilege. *Oxford Review of Education, 7*(2), 173–191.

Yeakey, C. C. & Bennett, C. T. (Winter, 1990). Race, schooling, and class in American society. *Journal of Negro Education, 59*(1), 3–18.

Chapter 3

THE HISPANIC-AMERICAN EXPERIENCE IN FAMILY CONTEXT

Hispanic families in the United States face many challenges to their survival and development (Carrasquillo, 1991; Valdivieso & Davis, 1988). In spite of these challenges, Hispanic parents show the desire to provide their children with the best moral and spiritual values and material means. These goals are achieved in more or less degrees due to the Hispanics' precarious socioeconomic experience in the United States. This chapter briefly describes the Hispanic experiences in the United States, emphasizing how they have affected the family and its role in the socialization and educational processes of their children. This chapter presents a frame of reference regarding the Hispanic family in the United States to objectively describe and evaluate Hispanic parents' involvement in the education of their children.

HISPANICS IN THE UNITED STATES

There is no uniform Hispanic family in the United States. Hispanic family types vary according to region, recency of immigration, level of education, and socioeconomic status. In addition, they represent a diverse configuration of backgrounds, skills, needs, and aspirations. The Hispanic population in the United States is mainly a community of first-, second-, and third-generation immigrants who have uprooted their families and left homes, friends, relatives, customs, food, and language for economic, political, professional, ideological, and educational reasons. These forces have pushed Hispanic immigrants from their home country and pulled them to the United States, because they had a sense of optimism toward the United States. In their homelands, the United States was advertised as a country in which resourcefulness, intelligence, and perseverance are rewarded. This description was reinforced by the economical and psychological support given by Hispanics already residing in the United States (Carrasquillo, 1991). However, many Hispanic immigrants find at their arrival that the United States is not the country that was described to them back in their homelands, and they begin to struggle in an inhospitable country with a different language, a different culture, and, in a way, different values and life styles.

The word *Hispanic* describes a heterogeneous group of people composed of clusters of ethnic groups whose priorities and concerns frequently differ from other minorities. Hispanics in the United States are mainly composed of Mexicans, Puerto Ricans, Cubans, Dominicans, Central and South Americans, and people of other Spanish origin groups. Each group is separately identifiable, but at the same time these groups share many similarities.

Hispanics of Mexican ancestry have long been the largest Hispanic group in the United States, representing about 58 percent of all Hispanic Americans. Mexican Americans reflect a variety of cultural patterns, including those created by their parental heritage and influenced by the time their families have been in the United States. There is also a significant group of Mexicans that is undocumented and do not share an adequate socioeconomic status in the United States. A significant percentage of Mexican-American school children in the Southwest have suffered academic failure because of the unwillingness or inability of schools to build a curriculum around their Spanish-speaking background (Moore & Pachón, 1985; Orum, 1988; U.S. Bureau of the Census, 1991).

Puerto Ricans constitute the second largest Hispanic group in the United States. In 1990, they represented 13 percent of the Hispanic population in the United States. They are concentrated in central cities, where their employment has mainly depended on the strength of the local manufacturing and service industries. Puerto Ricans are the poorest of all Hispanic families in the United States (U.S. Bureau of the Census, 1991). As U.S. citizens, and coming from a democratic country where English is taught as a second language and where educational attainment has surpassed most countries in Latin America, it is not easy to understand their high level of poverty in the United States. Their low wages, the decline of manufacturing and service jobs, and the high costs of urban living have contributed to their poor status in the United States (Institute for Puerto Rican Policy, 1989; Moore & Pachón, 1985). Circular migration from the island to the mainland and vice versa contributes to keeping hopes high and maintaining a sense of closeness and togetherness.

Cubans are the third largest national origin group in the United States, with 7 percent of the Hispanic population in the United States (U.S. Bureau of the Census, 1991). Cubans, in general, share a more favorable socioeconomic status. Many middle-class Cubans left Cuba at the beginning of the 1960s to escape from communism, and they have been able to transfer their educational and commercial skills and create a successful Cuban community in the United States. They have been successful in establishing themselves using their background knowledge and business skills and have been successful in businesses related to construction, real estate, clothing, tobacco, restaurants, television, and newspapers.

Dominicans constitute the fourth largest Hispanic group in the United States. While Dominicans have utilized legal immigration to the fullest, there is also a significant undocumented group residing in the United States. Dominicans come to the United States mainly in search of jobs. However, their hopes do not always materialize due to English language barriers or a lack of job skills. Parents of Dominican children share immediate social, educational, and economic needs: housing, jobs, English language competence, cultural adjustment, formal education or vocational training, and financial and legal assistance (Carrasquillo, 1991; Leavitt & Kritz, 1989).

Central and South Americans are among the most recent of the major immigrant streams. Many have come in search of a better life for their families, but they have also fled their countries due to the political disturbances there. Their exact numbers in the United States are difficult to estimate because of their undocumented status and because the census questionnaire does not differentiate among their national origins. The Latin American population has increased greatly and has become dispersed in recent years. Latin Americans live in large cities such as New York, Los Angeles, Miami, and Houston, but they also relocate to semirural areas.

The Hispanic American population—native and foreign born—continues to grow at a tremendous rate (U.S. Bureau of the Census, 1991). A large percentage of Hispanic families (with the exception of Cubans) are poor and are of a low socioeconomic status. Socioeconomic status is a broad concept: it encompasses not only social class but also education, occupation, income, and several other factors. Low socioeconomic status describes a consistent pattern of life: low level of education, unskilled and semiskilled work, low income, and residence in a poor area (Institute for Puerto Rican Policy, 1989; Moore & Pachón, 1985; U.S. Bureau of the Census, 1991; Valdivieso & Davis, 1988). In many instances, high socioeconomic status means that all elements are reversed. A high school education and the acquisition of certain social and employment skills are the usual prerequisites to secure a lower middle-class position. Unfortunately, most Hispanic families do not share middle-class life styles. The U.S. Bureau of the Census (1991) provided the following facts:

1. In 1990, the estimate of the Hispanic-origin population in the United States was about 20.8 million, or about 8.4 percent of the total population.
2. About 92 percent of Hispanic households were in urban areas. They were less likely to own or to be purchasing their home than were non-Hispanics.
3. Hispanic families differ from non-Hispanic families in composition and size. Families maintained by a female householder with no husband present were 23 percent of all Hispanic families, compared with 16 percent of non-Hispanic families.
4. Hispanic families on the average were larger than non-Hispanic families. Twenty-eight percent of Hispanic families had five or more members, compared with about half of this percentage for non-Hispanic families.
5. Hispanic-origin population is younger than the non-Hispanic population. About 30 percent of Hispanics were under age 15 compared with 21 percent of non-Hispanics.
6. Hispanics made modest gains in educational attainment. The proportion of Hispanics who had completed four years of high school or more was 51 percent.
7. Hispanic households tend to have lower incomes than non-Hispanics. In 1989, the median money income of Hispanic households was $21,900 compared with $29,500, for non-Hispanic households.
8. About 26.2 percent of Hispanic persons in the United States were living in poverty in 1989, compared to 11.6 percent of non-Hispanics.

Hispanics reflect a variety of cultural patterns, including those created by their parental heritage, by the length of time their families have been in the United States, and by the socioeconomic level they have achieved in the United States. There are general experiences shared by many Hispanic families in the United States, such as the Spanish language, family structure and characteristics, and Hispanic culture. Spanish language, religious beliefs, family structures, and general customs are enhanced among Hispanics. But, at the same time, Hispanic children represent a diverse group within a group in a country that does not value diversity but rather values uniformity through a common language, culture, and race (Carrasquillo, 1991). Hispanic children have a broad range of language characteristics and needs that impact upon their development.

Many individuals see the two-parent household as an ideal one. However, there are significant groups of Hispanic families living in a single-parent household (U.S. Bureau of the Census, 1991). In many Hispanic families, a woman is the head of the family; she is the only financial provider and the only moral and social support. Because many Hispanic families are headed by women, and because the female-headed, single-parent family is generally the most limited with respect to financial and personal resources, Hispanic families are often the families with the least financial and moral support.

But in spite of the limited resources, Hispanics put great emphasis on family relationships (Carrasquillo, 1991; National Council of la Raza, 1987). The word "family" includes not only the nuclear group of father, mother, and children but also the extended family of several generations, including cousins, uncles, and grandparents. The extended family is very common among Hispanic families where it is customary to see the grandmother, the mother's brother, an aunt, and a homeland neighbor living in the same apartment or house. Another common characteristic of the extended Hispanic family is seen in relatives or friends staying until they improve their economic situation or find their own apartment. Relatives are welcome to live with the families because in many cases they may represent a second salary for the household. Grandparents are likely to remain with the family and they are welcome. Grandparents are not seen as a burden, but as a blessing. This is due to their knowledge and their function as a role model for the children or as individuals who can take care of the children during the parent's absence (Carrasquillo, 1991; National Council of la

Raza, 1987). Often, grandparents are the only adults children see during the day and late at night. In general, what Hispanic parents expect from their children's education, to a large extent, is determined by the nature of their educational and economic experiences. Like the children of other minority groups, Hispanic children are frequently plagued by problems revolving around economic barriers and lack of understanding from the educational system. But Hispanic parents try to give their children the best they can offer.

As expected, there are social and cultural tensions between Hispanic parents and their children (Fitzpatrick, 1982). One reason is the clash between the parents' homeland's values and culture and the children's life styles. The children are raised in the American society and American schools where American values and life styles are presented and encouraged. Children are brought up with peers who share the same American life styles and these children tend to deviate from the traditional Hispanic life styles. At times, it looks as if the parents do not understand their children and the children do not understand their parents' culture (Fitzpatrick, 1982). The biggest conflict is during the children's adolescence, but after children become young adults they become more conscious of their ethnic and cultural roots. Also, parents have accommodated themselves and begun to accept certain children's life styles. A compromise is worked out between parents and children in which both sides show appreciation and respect for both cultures and life styles.

THE HISPANIC FAMILY

The family is the principal agent in children's socialization, although today, this function is being shared largely with the school. The family is still the primary agent in passing on social and learning skills. The child is almost totally in the care of the parents during the first few years of life when the basic learning characteristics of personality are being formed. Child bearing and child care also remain primary functions of the family. Families prepare children to aspire to a higher position in society and to feel good about themselves. The parents and the community need to work together in the child-rearing process such that each child's experience is unique and rewarding. The crucial relationship between parent and children significantly emphasizes the role of parents in this socialization and learning process (Otto, 1962). Though parents must play many roles within their own cultural group, in child rearing there are some responsibilities that are consistent across all cultural groups. Every child must be fed, clothed, kept warm and comfortable, touched, and involved in some type of communication to develop physically, emotionally, and socially. How children are cared for and reared varies across ethnic and cultural groups. For Hispanic children, the family and the home are their first and primary support system. Secondary support systems include the school, community centers, and, in some cases, the church. All of them work together to provide children with a nurturing environment.

Hispanic families are interested in the well-being of their children, but socioeconomic conditions in many instances do not allow them to fulfill their desire of providing the best for their children. The Hispanic family is poorer than the Anglo family. Hispanic children in two-parent families are twice as likely as children in two-parent Anglo families to live below the poverty level. Many Hispanic males are underemployed, and they cannot support their children and their families. Also divorce and separation are high among Hispanic migrants. Many fathers remain in the homeland and only the mother and children migrate to the United States (Carrasquillo, 1991). The poor living standards of many Hispanics have required a higher degree of home sharing and cooperation among Hispanic families.

Hispanic children are taught very early to respect their elders by bowing their heads. In the school, however, some teachers insist that students look at them when giving verbal responses. Other teachers fail to understand that illness in the family requires everyone to remain home until the sick person's health is restored. Ignorance of such cultural patterns or the inability to understand them results in unjustly labeling students as belligerent or docile or not interested in school. Many teachers do not only understand cultural differences; they are also insensitive to and often shocked by the accelerated social maturity of urban Hispanic children. Hispanic urban children become socially mature at an early age in order to survive in a hostile society and community. By the time the average Hispanic urban child is age 10 or 12, she or he has seen too much of the difficulties of life. Poverty, crime, and violence are all familiar to these children.

A PROPOSAL FOR HISPANIC PARENTAL INVOLVEMENT

If Hispanic parents are provided with positive information about their child's learning, they are more likely to participate in school-related activities. It is important to develop ideas, strategies, and procedures for establishing communication and trust with Hispanic parents. In some instances, parents' notions about the American school experience and how schools function are often limited, and they may have inaccurate perceptions about what social, cultural, and academic skills are required for academic success in the United States.

Many families arrive every year in the United States, and many children attend schools shortly after arrival. Most of them (both parents and children) experience cultural, social, and linguistic trauma. There are a variety of attitudes toward school that may limit the extent to which parents feel at ease playing active teaching roles. One way to attract Hispanic parents to the school decision-making process is by linking the life of the school with that of the Hispanic community, a community mainly interested in developing and improving the education of all children, but especially Hispanic children (Orum, 1988). Many times educators criticize Hispanic parents for their lack of involvement. But it is not that Hispanic parents are not concerned about their children's education; it is that these parents are preoccupied trying to cope with problems, such as learning English, finding housing, securing employment, and otherwise trying to survive in a very hostile society. Knowledge of the relationship between parents and their children will also reveal useful information about parents' aspirations for their children and how they communicate these aspirations.

Hispanic parents tend to see the school as the main force responsible for their children's education and academic development. Parents have an absolute trust in teachers and the school administration. In many instances, they do not question the quality of education their children receive because they feel they are not educationally prepared and equipped to question those who are better prepared than they to teach their children. Many times the school sees this sense of no direct involvement as "lack of interest and cooperation." It is not a lack of interest or cooperation; it is that Hispanic parents are afraid of intervening in teachers' functions and roles. Parents feel that they cannot tell the teachers how to teach their children. These parents are incapable of even questioning the teacher about any academic matter. However, when there is a social activity in the school and the school asks for the parents' cooperation, these parents put all their effort, time, and economic means to cooperate with the school. They bring in the best dishes to be shared by all attendees. Thus, socio-academic functions are enjoyed by Hispanic parents. At graduations, school assemblies, or special programs, Hispanic parents go all the way to make their children look well when participating in these activities. They document these memorable events in photographs and on videotapes because they want to record and keep these positive experiences of their own children in school. Many Hispanic parents do not have the necessary schooling to be able to sit down with their children and help them do their homework or help them in other school tasks (Orum, 1988). These parents feel uneasy if confronted with this situation and try to avoid these unhappy moments by not sitting down with their children (Carrasquillo, 1991). Furthermore, many of these parents do not have acadenic skills themselves so that if the child asks a specific question, they are unable to answer. Therefore, parents avoid this academic and embarrassing situation altogether. But this example does not mean that these parents do not care about their child's school progress. Hispanic parents do care, but they do not have the academic background to be helpful to the child. What the school needs to do is to provide these parents with the understanding that although they cannot sit down with the child and actually work on a school task, there are other ways in which these parents can help the child. Parents can discuss with their child how the teacher explained the homework; they can identify another student who can work with their child; or they can decide to learn along with the child. Because in many Spanish-speaking countries community involvement in school planning is not significant, many parents believe that it is right to place all responsibility for educating their children on school leaders. Such parents might not consider it appropriate to go beyond seeing that the children's homework is completed, requiring that the children behave well in school, or attending an open house.

Another important variable in evaluating parental-school involvement is that of the English language proficiency of Hispanic parents. There exists a large diversity of language background and language characteristics among Hispanic parents. Some of them are bilingually proficient in English and Spanish. Others are proficient in Spanish with a functional speaking knowledge of English. Some are English proficient with no knowledge of Spanish. A few are illiterate in both languages. The school needs to address these parents' language diversity and be prepared to come up with strategies to communicate with them in spite of their language diversity or English language limitations. Parents need to be able to understand the information that is sent to them by the school. A letter to parents must be written in both English and Spanish, and the language format and the content need to be simple and meaningful to them. Telephone calls and parent conferences need to follow the same approach. Parents need to feel that they are part of the school; they need to feel at ease with, not scared and mistrusting of, the school. A personal approach to parents will keep them close to school: informally inviting them to visit and observe classrooms, participate in social and cultural activities presented by their children, and volunteer to work in the different school programs. For example, parents can present workshops on how to make show puppetry, or they can teach the Spanish language or Spanish cooking, music, or dancing.

Hispanic parents need to be encouraged to be part of the community school board, the Parents' Association, and the community advisory boards so that they become active participants in the school's decision-making process: participating in final decisions pertaining to programs and approval of curriculum, hiring of school staff, and expenditure of the school budget. And the school needs to develop strategies to enable Hispanic parents to participate in these activities even if they are limited in their ability to use the English language.

There are numerous roles for parents and other community members to assume: learner, teacher, decision maker, advisor, community representative. As learners, parents can gain knowledge in such areas as individualized instruction, team teaching, and language development. As teachers they can become partners in their children's education. As decision makers, advisors, or community representatives, they can become active in school organizations.

The communication of expectations between parents and educators is seldom a one-way street. Educators, parents, and children all impact and change each other in different ways. The success of Hispanic communities will depend on the balance regarding the following issues:

- Teachers' and administrators' desire to learn about Hispanic parents' ethnic, cultural, and linguistic life styles;
- Parents' interests in learning about and awareness of school procedures, pedagogy, and children's academic/school development;
- Home reinforcement of academic development; and
- Parental influence on school programs and curriculum decisions.

Both Hispanic families and the school, teachers, and administrators need to be flexible in making changes to meet and satisfy students' needs. Both are partners in education.

In conclusion, Hispanic Americans are both the oldest and newest immigrants to the United States; they are special in their cultural and linguistic heritage, their traditions and skills and they represent an important resource to the United States. Hispanics in the United States seek social, economic, and educational opportunities for themselves and their children. Immigration policies in the United States have encouraged the entrance of people of Hispanic origin. Participation by parents in the education of their children has not been entirely successful due to social and language barriers. For many years, Hispanic parental involvement in education has been viewed negatively, and teachers were often even hostile to parents who wanted to participate.

Hispanic parents are realizing to a greater extent that they can also play an instrumental role in making decisions that affect their children. The key to this concept lies in the cooperative approach whereby administrators, teachers, parents, and, at appropriate times, students work collectively in making decisions. If educators are indeed concerned about the whole child and youth, and if they desire looking at the child and youth's social-emotional, cognitive, and physical development, then they must realize the important role that Hispanic parents can play. Hispanic parents are eager and willing to participate in educating their children cognitively, socially, emotionally, and physically.

REFERENCES

Carrasquillo, G. L. (1991). *Hispanic children and youth in the United States: A resource guide.* New York: Garland.

Fitzpatrick, J. (1982). Transition to the mainland. In Cordasco, E. & Buchioni, E. (Eds.), *The Puerto Rican community and its children on the mainland* (pp. 57–59). Metuchen, New Jersey: Scarecrow Press.

Institute for Puerto Rican Policy. (1989). *Towards a Puerto-Rican Latino agenda for New York City.* New York: Institute for Puerto Rican Policy.

Leavitt, J. & Kritz, M. (1989). *Three immigrant groups in New York City and human services: Dominican, Haitians, and Colombians.* New York: Community Council of New York.

Moore, J. L. & Pachón H. (1985). *Hispanics in the United States.* Englewood Cliffs, New Jersey: Prentice-Hall.

National Council of la Raza. (1987). *The Hispanic elderly: A demographic profile.* Washington, D. C.: National Council of la Raza.

Orum, L. S. (1988). Making education work for Hispanic Americans: Some promising community-based practices. Mimeographed Manuscript. Washington, D. C.: National Council of la Raza.

Otto, H. A. (1962). What is a strong family? *Marriage and Family Living,* 24, 72–82.

United States Bureau of the Census. (1991). *The Hispanic population in the United States: March 1990.* (Current Population Report,

Series P-20, No. 449). Washington, D. C.: Government Printing Office.

Valdivieso, R. & Davis, C. (1988). *U. S. Hispanics: Challenging issues for the 1990's*. Washington, D. C.: Government Printing Office.

Chapter 4

THE ASIAN-AMERICAN EXPERIENCE IN FAMILY CONTEXT

> We, Asian Americans and Pacific Island peoples, are the personification of an authentic pluralistic reality in America! You cannot lump us together. Each Asian or Pacific ethnic group stands out as distinctly and uniquely beautiful and vibrant. We affirm our individual ethnicity. We shall perpetuate our diversity. We shall be forever pluralistic. (Ignacio, 1976, pp. 121–122.)

The United States has absorbed immigrants from all corners of the world, who have brought with them different cultural values, religious beliefs, and languages. A book like this would not be complete without discussing family and educational characteristics of Asian Americans in the United States. Asian Americans, although not a homogeneous ethnic group, share family factors that need to be known and understood by educational policy makers and practitioners.

ASIAN-AMERICAN IMMIGRATION TO THE UNITED STATES

Although this chapter discusses Asian Americans as a group, it is important to say that this population may be the most diverse of U.S. major minority groups (Fawcet & Carino, 1987; O'Hare & Felt, 1991). Asians come from more than two dozen different countries of Asia and the Pacific Islands: China, Philippines, Japan, Korea, Vietnam, Samoa/Tonga/

Guam, Laos, Thailand, Cambodia, just to mention a few. They do not share a common language, a common religion, or a common cultural background.

It is difficult to separate Asians from Pacific Islanders. The definition of the U.S. Bureau of the Census describes an Asian or Pacific Islander as a person having origins in any of the original peoples of the Far East, Southeast Asia, the Indian subcontinent, or the Pacific Islands (U.S. Bureau of the Census, 1990). In this chapter, the term "Asian American" refers to individuals whose race or ethnicity is listed in that definition.

The United States has received immigrants from almost every country in Asia. It is not possible here to identify all the cultural, linguistic, and social contributions as well as the unique characteristics of all Asian immigrants, therefore, the discussion in this chapter focuses mostly on the groups with the most residents in the United States. There is a significant group of Asian-American residents in the United States or citizens whose ancestry is Chinese, Indochinese (Vietnamese, Laotians, and Cambodians), Filipino, Korean, and Japanese (U.S. Bureau of the Census, 1990). Social and economic pressures and in some cases political upheaval caused the early Asian immigrants to leave their respective homes. At the beginning of the 19th century, many Asians came to America to seek a better life. Others came to make enough money to be able to return to their families and live an easy life from their savings. Early Asian immigrants became easily vulnerable in the massive demand for cheap labor, and many of their dreams were never realized (Cheng, 1987; Woo, 1985). Still, they kept coming to the United States and most of them never went back. The pioneer Asian immigrants were mostly laborers, and they were predestinated to a life of poverty. Initially welcomed, they were soon exploited through cheap labor and repressed by unscrupulous business individuals (Chu-Chang, 1983; Ignacio, 1976).

During the 20th century, a massive wave of Asian immigration took place in the mid-1960s. The immigrants at this time were mostly from the Philippines, Korea, Taiwan, and Hong Kong. After the passage of the National Origin Act of 1965, which raised Asian immigration between 1965 and 1974, other ethnic groups from Asia became more noticeable. These groups of Asians were better trained and skilled and more experienced than earlier Asian immigrants. They settled in urban centers throughout the United States, but their life was hard because the established Asian populations resented their presence and competition (Woo, 1985).

The Asian population grew more rapidly than any other minority group in the 1980s, and there is every reason to believe that it will continue to grow at high rates during the 1990s (O'Hare & Felt, 1991). For purposes of clarifying distinctive historical and social perspectives of Asians, a brief historical overview of four Asian groups (Chinese, Japanese, Koreans, and Filipinos) in the United States follows, emphasizing that reasons and time of immigration of Asian groups vary.

The Chinese first emigrated to the United States almost two centuries ago. However, it was not until 1840, when the California gold rush precipitated the arrivals of large numbers of immigrants, that the Chinese started to emigrate in significant numbers. This was America's first major encounter with Asian immigrants. The Chinese came from different provinces in mainland China, and from Taiwan and Hong Kong. Most came primarily to study or to join relatives or other members of their families. In recent years, a significant number of Chinese immigrants have come to the United States for business purposes; others, especially from Hong Kong, because they fear the consequences of the Communist takeover of Hong Kong in 1997 (Woo, 1985).

There are many languages and dialects spoken in China. Many educators are not aware of these linguistic differences among the Chinese in the United States and when developing educational programs, such as bilingual educational programs, they may risk lumping all of them together (Chu-Chang, 1983). This linguistic diversity is reflected in the Chinese immigrant population in the United States. There is a large representation of Chinese Mandarin, Cantonese, and Wondaig speaking, which in many cases creates difficulties for the U.S. educational system and for the Chinese children and youth.

Japanese immigrants are the most established and rooted Asian-American group in the United States. Because land in Japan is limited, large numbers of Japanese farmers began to emigrate to the United States (first to Hawaii and then to California). Japanese first arrived in 1886 as contract laborers in Hawaii. During World War II, the Japanese encountered resentment and hostility. They lost their land and were imprisoned in the United States. In recent years, there has been a new steady influx of Japanese immigrants. The Japanese in the United States are highly educated; many have high school diplomas and college degrees. They have done well in the professional arena, and they are well off socially and economically.

Korean immigration to the United States started in 1903 in Hawaii. There, the Koreans worked as contract laborers before continuing their massive immigration to the mainland in 1904, mostly to the West Coast. The main reason for their immigration was the Japanese takeover and the Japanese military persecution and political upheavals. Many Koreans fled to the United States in pursuit of peace, freedom, and prosperity. By 1945, the United States and the Soviet Union made an agreement to surrender North Korea to the Soviet Union and South Korea to the United States. But, in 1950, North Korea invaded South Korea and the Korean War began; it lasted until 1953, bringing large numbers of new Korean immigrants to the United States. The dominant society on the U.S. mainland is ignorant of the essential differences between

North and South Koreans as well as those of other Asian-American ethnic groups.

Filipinos have long-term historical roots in the United States. The Philippines were ceded to the United States after Spain's defeat in the Spanish-American War. During World War II, when the Japanese were winning the war in the Pacific, the Japanese took over the Philippines. After winning World War II, the United States granted independence to the Philippines. Filipinos are a multigenerational, multicultural, and multilingual group. The Filipino population in the United States is composed of different cultural and linguistic groups (e.g., Tagalog, Ilocano, Pampangans, Bilocano, Visayan, and Zamboangueno) (Woo, 1985). It is common for a first-generation Filipino to speak Tagalog, Ilocano, and his or her native dialect plus English and Spanish.

During the 1980s, the Asian-American population grew by 80 percent. That rate of growth was six times higher than that of African Americans and twice as high as that of Hispanics (O'Hare & Felt, 1991). The 1990 U.S. Bureau of the Census estimated that 6.9 million Asians were living in the United States. Immigration from Asia has been promoted by: (1) current immigration policy emphasis on family reunification, (2) enactment of immigration legislation in 1990 increasing the total number of immigrants, and (3) preference given to individuals who have work skills needed by U.S. businesses.

Most recent immigrants from China, Korea, and the Philippines came to the United States due to family reunification. Many of them were highly educated and entered the United States under employment provisions of the immigration laws. There was a significant number of immigrants and refugees from some of the war-torn countries of Southeast Asia (Vietnam, Laos, Cambodia) who arrived in the United States as a result of U.S. policies following the end of the Vietnam War and unstable political and economic conditions in their home country (O'Hare & Felt, 1991).

There is no single Asian-American ethnic group (Fawcet & Carino, 1987). Each group mentioned above has its own distinct history, culture, language, art, religion, tradition, customs, values, demography, and life styles. Each group wishes to retain its respective ethnic communities where ethnic culture, values, and virtues are perpetuated and enriched. All of these groups, although living in the United States, maintain their language, culture, values, and life styles. They tend to stay together by settling in the same neighborhood or communities. Asian Americans are highly concentrated in the western region of the United States. The majority of Asian Americans live in metropolitan areas with about equal numbers living in central cities and suburbs. Half of them live in the following metropolitan areas: Honolulu, Los Angeles, Long Beach, San Francisco, Oakland, New York, Chicago, and San Jose (General Accounting Office, 1990; O'Hare & Felt, 1991; U.S. Bureau of the Census, 1990). Chinatowns throughout the United States have their economic base, and legitimate residents often profit from them. Chinatowns have become the political power base in dealing with the outside world. They are also the center of social and cultural life. The Japanese communities have built an economic base for themselves that has maintained their ethnic and cultural life as a unique group of people. This togetherness helps them to retain their ethnic character and identity.

Data on the socio-economic status of Asian Americans are scarce and give a mixed picture of their status. Recent immigration has brought two very distinct groups of Asians to the United States. One group is educated and ready to move into the mainstream quickly; the other lacks educational background and skills to move out of poverty (O'Hare & Felt, 1991). The average family income of Asian Americans is comparatively high, although their poverty rate has increased during the last decade. Poverty within the Asian-American community tends to be overshadowed by the high income of some Asian Americans. Yet, a large percentage of the Asian community lives in poverty. One of the most accepted reasons for this discrepancy is that the flood of new Asian immigrants may increase the poverty rate but many of the second and third generation of Asian immigrants may be moving up in socio-economic status.

More than three-quarters (76 percent) of Asian-American families live in married-couple families and only 5 percent live alone (O'Hare & Felt, 1991). Most Asian children grow up with the benefits of a two-parent family. In general, Asians tend to marry later and experience less marital disruption than the average population. Postponement of child bearing also contributes to economic well-being, increases opportunities for higher education, and leads to better paying jobs. Many Asians live in an extended family, in which a parent or a grown child or a brother or sister live in the same house.

All Asian-American groups have suffered the insensitivity of the American dominant culture to their self-fulfilling ethnic identities. Parents and school personnel should teach their children to respect other's diversity and ethnic autonomy and encourage each other's quest for their rightful place in society. Parents should teach their children to develop a pluralistic attitude in which respect for diversity is encouraged and praised.

THE ASIAN-AMERICAN FAMILY EXPERIENCE

Although it is improper to discuss generic family patterns of Asian Americans as if they were one ethnic group, the generalizations presented below have been found to be true for most Asian groups. (Many of these points are also applicable to other non-Asian ethnic groups.) It is common for people with no contact with other ethnic groups to erroneously assume that all ethnic groups are the same or assume that people from another culture are so different that communication with them is not possible. What parents and teachers need to inculcate in their children or students is that there are cultural and linguistic characteristics that are specific to the various ethnic groups and that there are many universal similarities especially related to human, moral, and educational development. Also, that differences do not mean deficiencies. On the contrary, these differences should be seen as factors that enrich the pluralistic culture of the United States.

Most Asian children have been raised in a very rigid, disciplined, and sheltered environment (Woo, 1985). One misconception about Asians is that they do not have emotions. All humans feel joy, anger, love, and hatred. But individuals differ in the way they express their emotions. It is said that Chinese hide emotions. The main reason for this misconception is that for the Chinese the most important value in social interaction is to preserve harmony rather than assert individuality (Woo, 1985). In traditional China, the basic unit is the extended family and not the individual. For a large number of family members living together in close proximity, it is imperative to maintain harmony. This does not mean that the Chinese do not show emotion, it is just that they are not demonstrative and outspoken. Another aspect of seeking to live harmoniously with other Asians is the need to be humble. For example, Asian individuals do not talk about their strengths because to do so would not be showing humbleness (Woo, 1985). Parents do not praise or acknowledge their children in public, thereby showing a humble attitude toward their children, and always expect their children to do better than they are presently doing. Also, most Asians tend to prefer to use a minimum of oral communication (Wei, 1983; Woo, 1985).

Linguistically and culturally, Asian Americans reflect a great diversity. For example, most Chinese students entering American schools are from the People's Republic of China and

Vietnam. The majority are still Cantonese speaking. However, there is also a sizable Mandarin-speaking minority from Taiwan and other provinces of China. A significant percentage of children from Cambodia speak Swatowese. Teaching Asian students can be an extremely complicated undertaking, and the resources and strategies teachers should put together and practice are extremely important.

Some Asian families immigrate with unrealistic expectations of what life in the United States will be like. After they arrive, they find that they have to work hard and are forced to take jobs far below their level of education. Many families have unemployed members, which is a blow to these members' self-respect and a bad influence on their home and family lives.

A problem among many Asian immigrant families is that the parents have to work long hours and are seldom at home. Their children are then forced to be more independent than they would have been in Asia. Children have to take care of themselves and of their younger brothers and sisters. Some of them also have to work after school, either at the family business or elsewhere. This may cut the children's studying time and may affect performance at school. Some view this situation as a challenge, a chance to develop self-determination and experience human fulfillment, to rise above the difficulties, while others are not as strong and may suffer from this situation.

School authorities, especially the teacher, are highly respected and their advice or orders are strictly followed. The teacher has a great authority. In many Asian schools, students must stand up and bow to the teacher to show respect and reverence when the teacher enters or leaves the classroom. Used to accepting the teacher's word as the final authority, students want to listen only to what the teacher has to say. Some would not question a teacher's word. The teacher's instructions are to be obeyed and never challenged. But, in a way, it is paradoxical that in spite of the great authority of the teacher, Asian-American students are less dependent on teachers than their American counterparts.

IN SEARCH OF EDUCATIONAL EXCELLENCE

Asians have always placed great emphasis on education (Chen & Stevenson 1989; Chu-Chang, 1983; Woo, 1985). Although traditionally their educational goals have been ethical and philosophical, social and educational changes have demanded more technical education. National economical weaknesses have made many Asian countries push their people, especially their children, to be determined to excel in science, technology, and mathematics. Asians see the goal of education as the training of people to obtain the skills and required degrees or diplomas to be fully employed. Thus, academic, technical, and vocational training is important.

Asian students are pushed to excel in schools (Woo, 1985; Yao & Kierstead, 1984). The traditional role of tests in achieving promotion or academic progress has placed a tremendous emphasis on examination preparation. For most parents, the most important subjects are reading, writing, and mathematics. Parents make sure that when their children are at home they are practicing these subjects. Asian parents praise teachers and expect them to assign a great deal of homework, especially in the above three areas. Asian-American students in general do not fear mathematics as much as Americans do. They have been told to practice, memorize, and drill on it until they become proficient on the subject. In general, Asian Americans consider being good in mathematics something to be proud of and parents want their children to excel in it.

Asian Americans have a great respect for scholastic work: degrees and diplomas are valued (Chen & Stevenson, 1989; Woo, 1985). One reason that a degree is so valued is that in most countries in Asia, there are far fewer universities to satisfy the demand for higher education and a university education is for the academic elite. Therefore, the competition to enter universities is intense and examinations are the keys for university acceptance. Such intense pressure has resulted in sending students to tutorial training and other test preparatory courses.

In Asian countries, the educational system promotes passivity; students learn by listening, reading, observing, and imitating rather than by engaging in independent thinking. Asian education places a great emphasis on memorization. For example, in mathematics, the rules of arithmetic are given, and the students either memorize them or have them drilled into them through exercises. The multiplication tables, for instance, are memorized as part of a routine. In regular lessons, the texts are frequently memorized. Teachers' lectures are memorized and reproduced during examinations. This is reinforced by the need to train students to pass examinations. It is common to see Asian-American students doing exceptionally well in American schools, especially if the above aspects are expected outcomes of the educational system. Students seldom ask questions in class, and teachers do not generally encourage students to ask questions.

Asian-American students prefer individuality over group interaction. Many of them do not like to be forced to speak in front of the whole class; they are afraid of saying something wrong. Many of them prefer to study on their own. Class participation and discussion are not part of the daily Asian school routine.

Figure 1 summarizes the Asian attitudes toward education and the educational implications of educating Asian students in the U.S. system.

The observations presented in Figure 1 do not mean that Asian-American students find everything easy in the educational system of the United States. Most of their educational problems are compounded by language problems

Figure 1

Asian Attitudes Toward Education

Asian Cultural Themes	*Educational Implications*
Education is a formal process.	Students learn by observation and by memorization. Pattern practice and rote learning are "studying."
Teachers are to be highly respected.	Children are to respect adults.
Humility is an important virtue.	Children must respect authority. Teachers have authority and control.
Reading of factual information is valuable study.	Rote learning is preferred over discovery learning.
It is important for students to be orderly and obedient.	Teachers carry knowledge and transmit information.
Schooling is a serious process.	Rote memory is an effective teaching tool. Homework in pattern practice is important and is expected.
Harmony is an important virtue.	Children are expected to listen to adults.
Filial piety is highly valued.	Teachers are not to be challenged or questioned.

Students are to engage in serious academic work.	The class is run in an orderly manner and is highly controlled.
Teachers are to behave formally and are expected to lecture and provide information. Students are reluctant to ask questions.	Students do well in sheltered and structured activity—less peer interaction and group projects, more lectures and instruction.
Students are not to "show off" or volunteer information.	Students are expected to work in a quiet environment and are not to roam freely around the classroom.
Reading fiction is not considered serious study.	Students avoid confrontation.
Students are to sit quietly and listen attentively.	Children are obedient.

Source: L.L. Cheng. (1987). *Assessing Asian Language Performance: Guidelines for Evaluating Limited English Proficient Students*, p. 14.

and basic learning styles. In terms of language, they may not understand the content presented in the classroom or be able to express what they want to say due to language limitations. Some Asian students do not do well on tests and examinations in English because they lack English language proficiency. Many Asian students are shy and afraid to speak before an audience. Asian children are taught to respect older people, deal with others peacefully, observe proper manners, and remember that making money is not the only purpose of education. In Asia, students are silent unless they are spoken to. In the United States, they are expected to initiate

higher grades. All these factors
er educational performance.

DOES PARENTAL INVOLVEMENT EXIST AMONG ASIAN PARENTS?

Asian Americans should not be viewed as a uniform group in terms of adjustment to and assimilation in American society. Many factors affect each person and each ethnic group. Some parents are more cosmopolitan than others and their attitudes are frequently reflected by their children. However, there are some general characteristics of or attitudes toward education that are not understood by American teachers. Cheng (1987) has listed some of these incongruities in Figure 2.

Asian parental involvement does exist, although not in the American style. In general, Asian parents do not interfere in school administration or educational policies and tend to follow the guidelines and rules established by the school. Asian parents do not challenge the school rules and are willing to accept them. However, these Asian parents' attitudes are changing, and Asian parents are now attending general parent meetings more frequently and are expressing their content or discontent with American schools. Asian parents cooperate by sending their children to school on a regular basis and pushing children to excel in school. This is done in several ways, such as through drilling their children, helping them to memorize, sending them to tutoring programs, or asking them to stay at home and study all the subjects learned in school and do the necessary homework.

Asian parents may view any request for school personnel for a conference as problematic. They often interpret such a request as an indication that their children are misbehaving at school and may feel embarrassed and ashamed. They may

Figure 2

Incongruities Between American Teachers' Expectations and Asian Parents' Expectations

American Teachers' Expectations	Asian Parents' Expectations
Students need to participate in classroom activities and discussion.	Students need to ask questions.
Students need to be creative.	Reading is a way of discovering
Students learn through inquiries and debate.	Students are to be quiet and obedient.
Asian students generally do well on their own.	Students should be told what to do.
Critical thinking is important.	Students learn through memorization and observation.
Analytical thinking is important.	Teachers need to teach; students need to "study."
Creativity and fantasy are to be encouraged.	It is important to deal with the real world.
Factual information is important; fantasy is not.	Teachers are not to be challenged.
Students should be taught the steps to solve problems.	Reading is decoding of information.

Source: L.L. Chang. (1987). *Assessing Asian Language Performance: Guidelines for Evaluating Limited English Proficient Students, p. 14.*

feel uncomfortable at such meetings, being unfamiliar with the social, linguistic, and cultural environment of the school. It is the school's responsibility to make Asian parents feel at ease in the American educational system.

In summary, most Asian cultures place a heavy emphasis on education and hard work, and children and youth are expected to pursue educational opportunities. But Asian Americans want to be understood and accepted and to have the same opportunities as other U.S. residents. This means effective and adequate education for their children, and an education that also values their language and their culture and is able to prepare them to live effectively with their own integrity. It also means elimination of prejudice and racism to channel Asian Americans into well-paying occupations that promote upward mobility. The realization and fulfillment of these needs are necessary to assure productive participation and contribution of the Asians in the United States.

REFERENCES

Chen, C. S. & Stevenson, H. W. (1989). Homework: A cross cultural examination. *Child Development, 60*(3) 551–560.

Cheng, L. L. (1987). *Assessing Asian language performance: Guidelines for evaluating limited English proficient students.* Rockville, Maryland: Aspen Publishers.

Chu-Chang, M. (Ed.). (1983). *Asian and Pacific-American perspectives in bilingual education.* Comparative research. New York: Teachers College Press.

Fawcet, J. T. & Carino, B. V. (Eds.). (1987). *Pacific Ridges: The new immigration from Asia and the Pacific Islands.* New York: Center for Immigration Studies.

General Accounting Office. (1990). *Asian Americans: A status report. Fact sheet for the chairman. Select committee on hunger. House of Representatives.* GAO-HRD-90 36FS, pp. 43–46. Washington, D.C.: Government Printing Office.

Ignacio L. F. (1976). *Asian American and Pacific islanders. Is there such an ethnic group?* San Jose, California: Philipino Development.

O'Hare W. P. & Felt, J. C. (1991). *Asian Americans: America's fastest growing minority group.* Washington, D.C.: Population Reference Bureau.

United States Bureau of the Census. (1990). *Money income and poverty status in the United States: 1989.* (Current population reports, Series p. 60, No. 168.) Washington, D.C.: Government Printing Office.

Wei, T. T. D. (1983). The Vietnamese refugee child: Understanding cultural differences. In Omarh, D.R. & Erichson, J.G. (Eds.), *The bilingual exceptional child* (pp. 197–212). San Diego, California: College-Hill Press.

Woo, J. W. T. (1985). *The Chinese-speaking student: A composite profile.* Unpublished paper. New York Board of Education.

Yao, E. L. & Kierstead, F. D. (1984). Can Asia educational systems be models for American education?: An Appraisal. *NASSP Bulletin,* 68 (476), 82–89.

Chapter 5

COMMUNITIES OF EDUCATION

The concept of "community" is basically an encompassing one and difficult to define. In a very peripheral way, Getzels (1978) talks of such factors as the neighborhood in which the school is located; the families whose children attend the school, even if they do not live in the immediate neighborhood; the administrative district responsible for operating the school; the political entity whose taxes support the school; and the communion of minds that are obviously reflected in a sense of "spirit." Because a school's community may be perceived as all of these publics and more, it is prudent to consider other extensions which include the geographic community, the smaller neighborhood construct in which children's homes are located: that is, the two-block area or street corner where children and youth hang out with friends; the academic community that provides professional personnel; the philanthropic community that supplies private funds to help operate special school projects; the political entity—city, town, or village—that may underwrite the supplies and also subsidize some other efforts through public funds; in essence, family-community links of moving and multiple associations that provide a cluster of social usages (Bronfenbrenner, 1979).

COMMUNITIES OF EDUCATION: CONCEPTS DEFINED

"Communities of education" derive their legitimacy from the function of their existence. School systems, school districts, schools and, therefore, communities of education and their programs are not neutral. In fact, whatever they are, they all exist in a highly charged political arena. For example, because schools have more contact with children than any other social institution (excluding the family), and because they are the single agency most amenable to public manipulation, the groups that organize and control the school also have a profound impact on indoctrination and training of future generations. Weber's (1947) substantive sociological position has long added credence to the view that it is possible to tell a great deal about power structure and patterns of social differentiation in a society if one can determine how schools and schooling are organized; how the content and process of schooling are dispensed; and, who benefits from attendance (Evans, 1962).

But a distinction must be made here between education and schooling. Cremin (1978) defines education as the deliberate, systematic, and sustained effort to transmit, evoke, or acquire knowledge, attitudes, values, skills, and sensibilities, and any learning that results from the effort, direct or indirect, intended or unintended. Broadly defined, education refers to the process of learning that happens over the span of one's entire life. According to Dewey (1938), it is a continuous, ever-changing process. Much of it does not take place in formal institutions. Humans begin their education at birth and continue it throughout life in a great variety of formal and informal settings. Education as a process is concerned with individual and psychological processes involved in learning and cognition. Here, psychology is the primary discipline that concerns itself with these processes, and psychologists specialize in the study of how individuals learn (Spring, 1991).

Schooling, on the other hand, is a social group process and sociology is its associate discipline. Sociology is concerned with the study of social groups, and the sociology of education is the study of groups of people within educational institutions. Sociologists have named the process of learning through which people pass while attending school as the "process of schooling" (Bennett & Le Compte, 1990). This process is concerned with three understandings that people, generally children, acquire as they participate in formal institutions whose specific function is the socialization of designated groups within society. Thus, sociologists also study the characteristics of people and institutions which make up educational systems, as well as the dynamics of their interaction and operations (Hobbs, 1978).

From the perspective of the practice called education, there is the process—variously called socialization, acculturation, enculturation, development, and learning—which takes place in all societies. However, in looking at the functions of schooling, it should be noted that they turn on the basis of well-defined theoretical assumptions about education. This implies that positions, ideological or philosophical, find their figure and ground on statements of interrelated sets of assumptions and propositions which help to explain perceptions of the world. These assumptions, operating as ways of explanations and organization, serve as mental road maps, guiding the way in which theorists perceive of the world (Goetz & Le Compte, 1984).

The positions held by theorists regarding the function of education and schooling are many and varied, yet they constitute a theoretical framework; that is, a set of related theories that serve as an overall way to explain, interpret, or investigate the educational world. The purpose of schooling, for example, gets rooted in the ideological discourse on theories of education and learning, often, with the discourse oscillating between two powerful ideological issues of social transmission and socialization, which undergird the sociology of education. And, here it becomes reasonable to explore this relationship within the dynamic, sociology of education (Davies, 1987; Evans, 1962; National Governors' Association, 1986).

SOCIOLOGY OF EDUCATION

One primary, theoretical issue addressed under the rubric of the sociology of education involves the concepts of social transmission and socialization. By this is meant a process by which a society's ways of life, values, beliefs, and norms or standards for appropriate behavior are transmitted from one generation to the next. In a traditional functionalist view of social transmission, each generation is supposed to pass on to each succeeding generation the rules and regulations, habits, and appropriate behaviors for operating in the society. This is the ideal. The task of individuals is to learn and accept their roles from within the society. The organization of social roles that members assume within society is referred to as the social structure (Coleman, 1987; Davies, 1987; Henderson, 1988).

Theories of transmission are concerned with the description of the structural aspects of the society and their transmission from one generation to the next (Parsons, 1951, 1959; Weber, 1947). Here, the theories are more concerned with how existing social structures facilitate the general function of society than with the role of change or societal transformation. As such, a sociological analysis, based on transmission theory, may examine the social system within a school in order to understand how the values and behaviors of the society are passed on. Values of the United States taught in schools in the spirit of neatness, efficient use of time, and obeying authority, for example, are supposed to be daily class routines (Dewey, 1938).

However, primary differences between theoretical frameworks concerned with transmission and those addressing transformation are explained by Weiler (1988) in terms of production and reproduction of culture. Reproduction of transmission is concerned with an examination of the ways in which existing social structures are exactly copied from one generation to the next. But, by contrast, theories of production, or transformation, give the specific activities and desires of individuals an important role in the creation of culture (Bennett & Le Compte, 1990). These two seemingly competing demands, or foci, have generated disparate sets of actions and responses as school people wrestle with the purpose of schooling.

PURPOSES OF PUBLIC SCHOOLING

Public schooling has become a central as well as a controversial institution of society. For example, parents select housing in terms of available schooling; politicians capitalize on their options to voice opinions on school issues; bigotry, racism, and discrimination take place easily at school buildings; conflict and violence occur as some parents accuse schools of not being patriotic, while others brand them guilty of flag-waving; some argue that school will end poverty, discrimination, segregation, and inequity, while others contend that schools by reason of their structure and function, perpetuate these problems and that there are people in the larger ecological environment who feed off of these societal discrepancies.

Within the context of these contrasting views and perceptions, discussion of public goals of schooling is basically divided into political, social, and economic goals (Spring, 1991). In general, political goals refer to the attempts to use educational systems to mold future citizens, maintain political stability, and shape political systems. Social goals include attempts to reform society, provide social stability, and give direction to social development. Economic goals involve the use of the public school system to sort and select talent for the labor market, develop human capital, and plan economic development. It is important, however, to recognize that these categories often overlap. For instance, the goal of eliminating poverty through schooling can be considered an economic as well as a social goal. The fact is, however, that in the final analysis, it is the prescribed goals conceptualized, designed, and developed at the higher levels of the state and district that get articulated at the level of the community school unit. So, a major question is, how will these goals get played out and supported in families and communities that act as educators?

FAMILIES AND COMMUNITIES AS EDUCATORS

The concept of "families and communities as educators" is very diverse. The existence of variant perspectives highlights the point that the more one looks at the family, or any other institution for the matter, the more it takes on a different meaning from the perspective of different frameworks. For this reason, therefore, it is useful to examine a variety of concepts that may help in defining institutions, when looking at their relationships across clusters of social usage, within the context of the human linkages, and in trying to understand the organization of the individual's life experience.

A point of issue is the notion that the same diversity of meaning that one may find in the various analytic approaches to the family may also be found in institutions if one carefully examines the meaning of the term. On the one hand, institutions have been defined as a cluster of social usages, indicating a way of thought and action of some prevalence or permanence (Appel, 1985; Leitcher, 1978). Such prevalence or permanence is often observed to be embedded in the habits of a group or the customs of a people. On the other hand, any formal organization (e.g., the government, the church, the university, the corporation, the trade union) may also be seen as an institution.

Like concepts of family and institution, the concept of community varies too, depending on whether the investigator or the participant definition is employed, and the extent to which this distinction is explicitly recognized. In considering the possible images of relationships among institutions that educate, the concept of community itself is significant, since the manner in which the community is defined has important consequences for the clustering of institutions that one may include within one's examination.

The community has been defined in a variety of ways, depending on the perspective and purpose. Here, in our instance, community has been defined in many of its variants to mean physical place (e.g., the place within a geographic boundary, such as a school district within a city limit). Community has also been defined in terms of functional relationships among institutions, which carry out certain economic functions. It has been defined in terms of sentiments (e.g., a sense of belonging or a sense of common heritage). In another sense, community has been defined in terms of time dimensions (e.g., a common history of interactions and memories). In fact, there appears to be a large number of ways in which a community may be defined. For this book, community implies the institutions whose basic functions are carried out and is not limited to the special community or the neighborhood; it includes people, religious institutions, schools, and formal, social, civic, and parochial organizations related to the ethnic or global social structures.

In a similar way, the concept of system is useful in attempting to understand relationships among institutions that educate, since it is the system that offers a perspective on how one area of social life or existence is related to another. This factor calls for the inclusion of the concept of configuration, which refers to institutional clusterings and, thereby, serves to define the relationships among institutions that educate.

The use of the systems concept implies that the relationship of the family to the school or to any other institution that educates cannot be adequately understood by merely looking at the contacts between the family and the school and other institutions, per se. For a substantive understanding of a systems concept, one must also inquire into other influences that affect the family, the school, and other related institutions. It also implies that the relation of the family to the school or other institutions may change considerably over time and that the process of negotiations between the family and the school must be understood. This is crucial to the process of fulfilling the educational goals and objectives of the child. In a particular sense, how these systems and institutions function as educators must be understood, because it is the nature of their dynamic linkages that in large measure ascertains the degrees of freedom in interaction among and between these several publics as they implicitly or explicitly service the child (Coleman, 1987; Getzels, 1978; Rich et al., 1979).

LINKAGES

At the heart of the several concerns is the issue of linkage, the dynamic link that transcends the mere physical and is used in the broader sense to imply or refer to the nature of connections among the several institutions that educate. Within a complex urban industrial society, the variety of institutions that may form an educational configuration is considerable. Huge urban centers, such as New York, Chicago, Los Angeles, and Philadelphia, require that one also look for different subgroups within the social structure (Parsons, 1951, 1959).

In particular, among large urban complexes, one important form of linkage among institutions occurs when there is overlapping membership. This is a basic feature of organizations as well as among families. Today, it is commonly recognized that the institution called the family has assumed a variety of configurations, not only in the United States, but elsewhere in the world. The term now has many varied meanings, going from a monogamous, nuclear family of husband, wife, and children, to an extended family construct with the wife's mother residing in the household and no husband present, to polygamous marriages. Those in a nuclear family of husband, wife, and children are linked to the families of origin of both husband and the wife, because the husband is, during the life cycle, a member of both his family of origin and his family of marriage. In the same way, the wife is simultaneously a member of both her family of origin and her family of marriage (Parsons, 1951, 1959; Weber, 1947).

Between these two extremes are several variations, defined in terms of activities, household unit, emotional closeness, symbolic construction, or more genealogical connections of distant relatives. Other caregivers in comparable contexts may face similar circumstances. The family is linked to the school because the child goes daily from family to school and back. The child, therefore, is at the same time a family member and a student at the school. Thus, varying from one stage of life to another, especially as significant historical changes take place, boundaries in a family remain, with the family, even in traditional forms, rarely if ever, encompassing the totality of the individual's life (Leitcher, 1978).

Ideally, the family as educator assumes that education takes place on a wide range of participant subscribers in configurations that overlap and have their own unique characters. These several participant subscribers facilitate a wide range of institutions. In addition to other families, there are schools, museums, religious institutions, places of work, hospitals, and community centers in a variety of settings within an organizational, life-long process, on multiple levels, often simultaneously occurring with differing content of learning and teaching, in which exists an intertwined fare of affective and cognitive treatment. All of these various institutions constitute a child's ecological environment, which must at the same time include what surrounds the school, forming the school community.

THE CHILD AND
THE SCHOOL COMMUNITY

Given all of the preceding circumstances, it stands to reason that when children enter school, they bring all of their personal and community environment influences. We cannot separate the way a child lives from the way a child learns. For children to learn and develop well, their entire community (i.e., parents, institutions of higher learning, other educational and cultural institutions, religious institutions, business, law enforcement agencies, volunteer and civic organizations, and social service and health agencies) must all be engaged in a partnership with the school. This means in an implicit or explicit manner.

Taking a cue from the African adage, "it takes a whole village to raise a child," it requires a living, growing network of mutual support for the child's whole development, whether this development implies educational, social, or personal efforts to improve, the results of schooling must begin with the needs of children. The school itself must be a cohesive community that agrees on its own needs and goals. Both the school and the larger community must cooperate in order to motivate children to learn, to support children in their learning, to instill work habits, and to reward achievement. This is crucial.

Community and school collaboration that aims to improve schooling outcome must require that

1. Community members, organizations, and agencies work with one another and together with schools in order to create and maintain a safe, wholesome environment for children.
2. The community as a whole show respect for children's achievement in school.
3. All participants work together to create a sense of neighborhood in which each member, including every child, is known and respected.

4. Members of the community convey their expectations that children will behave appropriately and responsively.
5. Members of the community help children to gain maturity and responsibility by affording them opportunities for service.

Unquestionably, pulling these efforts together must mean a concerted effort which derives its leadership from all publics, beginning with the wise and dedicated involvement of school districts, school boards, and schools in which their own sense of innovation, change, and flexibility must be made manifest. Talk is not enough. The curriculum offered, for example, must be designed to excite and motivate students such that school will present itself as a place where children will want to hurry to and stay at for extended periods because what goes on there captures their interest and imagination.

SCHOOL DISTRICTS AND SCHOOL BOARDS

In the dynamic change that is sweeping the nation in terms of demographics, there must be a resultant reaction in schools. As the population changes in a dramatic world of change, school people must shift gears and meet those compelling needs that come with time. Signals coming in from the international arena with concerns about competition for world goods and services that are frequently translated in economic and trade terms suggest the futility of school people to overlook the implications. Prudence dictates that new curricula among other needs should lead the way as a call to upgrade schooling as needs change.

As school districts throughout the nation become stimulated, Banks (1981) suggested over a decade ago, that in view of the rational need and impending international challenge, the nation must move beyond its piecemeal response to private support to that of stimulation from social forces and, instead mount a substantive, wide-ranging curriculum reform movement, something of the likes of the post-Sputnik era. The nation still awaits that thrust, despite the rhetoric coming from diverse charters respecting "good" intentions. Thus, while there are piteously few small efforts at curricular reform, much of the dialogue is stymied in the diatribe of political persuasion, in which there is much disagreement and seeming confusion about what these reforms should be designed to attain and what proper relationships these reforms should facilitate given the growing multicultural character of student population across the land.

Educators and social scientists who embrace divergent views and ideologies find themselves offering conflicting school and curricular policies. There is still the difficulty of marrying the conflicting ideologies of the pluralists and assimilationists and, extrapolating the best of both worlds from these positions. A middle ground is a feasible way to proceed, but it is part of a larger political interest of maintaining the control of power in traditional hands. A curriculum that meets the needs and interests of a new United States, while preparing would-be-citizens with the qualitative wherewithal that would allow them to compete with their counterparts across the globe, still remains an option that awaits investment, serious investment (Walburg, 1984; Weiler, 1988).

SCHOOL BOARDS AND BOARDS OF EDUCATION

While the nation grapples with a consensus for curricular change, there is much that local constituent bodies, managements of the educative responsibility and process, can and should be doing. Taking the lead from the state authority, local school boards and school systems are duly bound to educate the citizenry. This is actualized in the school unit, the place of teaching and learning. Let us look at the school boards of education.

School boards are expressions of the democratic ideal of enabling ordinary, lay persons to decide on what is considered best for themselves and their children. The idea of school boards is rooted in a 200-year-old tradition of lay control of public schools. As such, school boards validate educational decisions with their legal authority, as well as their responsiveness to the community's will. They do not administer, but rather exert their leadership role by formulating policy and evaluating performance. They guide the core purposes and shape the values of the institution they serve. Through policy, school boards define school district missions and performance standards.

As a practical matter, school boards reflect and guide the will of the community, transforming it into policies, programs, and services for the young. But this is only part of the overall function. They also have an array of legal responsibilities that include establishing rules for student order and discipline, as well as prescribing courses of study and textbooks to be used; purchasing school sites; hiring teachers; and raising funds. In essence, the law charges school boards with the responsibility for the superintendence, management, and control of the educational affairs at the district level.

Boards of education manage to perform their many tasks by committees. Many responsibilities are delegated to administrators or shared with teachers, parents, and other community participants. But they are held accountable for all outcomes produced by decisions they share. As community members charged with responsibility for overseeing the operation of local public school systems, school boards play a vital role. And they function most effectively when:

1. They adhere to their policy-making role, delegating the administration of the schools and holding accountable those to whom they delegate responsibility.
2. They provide the resources that are necessary for allowing all pupils to achieve state goals and desired learning outcomes.

3. They develop opportunities for everyone—meaning staff, students, and community organizations—to participate meaningfully and purposefully in the educational enterprise (New York State Education Department, 1991, p. 1).

These several administrative and legal caveats are then filtered to school units where they are actualized as classroom activities and responsibilities. In this sense, the school as a unit, takes on exceptionally crucial functions.

THE SCHOOL

In the U.S. educational system, the primary operating unit for dispensing educational goods and services is the individual school. The complex of students, parents, staff, and community (inclusive of religious bodies, industries, and government) has a distinctive culture of its own. That is to say, a distinctive culture in the way of doing things, in its interpersonal relationships, and in attitudes toward learning held by children, parents, teachers, and others. The school, therefore, is not only a place of instruction; it may also be considered a custodial caregiver, an arena in which values are cultivated, acquired, and exchanged. It is also, an accrediting agent, a place where young people spend most of their waking hours, and, perhaps, the single social institution most likely to affect the development of most children (Bennett, 1988; Spring, 1991).

An individual school then, by definition, must be perceived as an institution with awesome responsibility which should be autonomous within the context of shared purpose and support. This autonomy appears to find its sustenance in shared operating decisions made by the principal, teachers, and other staff members, as well as by parents. It is a dynamic expression of site-based decision making, not simply as an erstwhile fad, but as a sound and enduring principle of institutional effectiveness. This implies that the school must be the primary unit of accountability, attending to the educational progress of individual students and the effectiveness of their individual teachers and other support systems in helping students acquire desired learning outcomes (Silber, 1989).

But schools and schooling take their primary responsibilities from larger agencies; first, from the school district which accepts greater charges from the state and legally assumes the right to educate the citizen. Thus, in our public system of elementary and secondary schools, the chief responsibility is seeing that students' learning is entrusted to local schools and school districts. While the state may establish goals and directions; provide resources, incentives, and assistance; and monitor progress and assess results, it cannot teach students (Schaps & Solomon, 1990).

Teaching students is a local responsibility, even within school districts, in the sense that learning ultimately depends more on what happens in classrooms. It is at the local level that school districts and schools exercise initiative to make what changes may be needed to bring about the learning results that are desired. Hence, in the unique relationship between state and localities, the state defines more precisely what is to be learned, and local teachers, staff, administrators, and boards of education have more freedom to decide how such teaching and learning should occur.

In essence, as the state spells out goals and desired learning outcomes; provides resources, incentives, and support; assesses progress; rewards successes; and remedies failures, boards of education, teachers, administrators, and parents have more to say about school organization and operation, instructional practice, pupil scheduling and grouping, staffing patterns, use of time, and other cogent matters. Accordingly, given the current exigency of new, innovative, and compelling demands of modernity, it is now projected that local school districts will perform the following functions in improving elementary, middle, and secondary schooling: (1) set local objectives and performance standards;

(2) provide resources, incentives, and assistance; and (3) exercise initiative to develop and conduct educational programs that produce better results (New York State Education Department, 1991, p. 141).

SCHOOLS AND PARENTAL PARTICIPATION

Despite the many innovative ideas conceptualized to meet compelling needs of schools and schooling, there is now a gradual attention toward including parents in the dynamic function of educating children and youth. Although many noticeable efforts have been made to dissuade parental participation in the affairs of schooling, there is a growing feeling that if given an honest, substantive opportunity, many parents can indeed provide needed assistance that transcends traditional peripheral responsibilities. Many school people have argued that many parents lack the know-how and preparation to operate professionally in schools. The recent little support there is for parents in schools has come largely from serious studies that justify their presence (Coleman, 1987; Cremin, 1978; Gough, 1989; Johnston & Slotnik, 1985; Sobol, 1987; Ungar, 1988; Weiler, 1988).

Although some evidence shows that the efficacy of the home in fostering learning has apparently declined for several decades, Walburg (1984) has demonstrated through his research that cooperative partnership between home and school can dramatically raise educational productivity. This study has been supported by Johnston & Slotnik (1985), two veterans of the wars in support of parent participation. They reviewed the ways and means of analyzing parents in the work of the schools and concluded that the benefits are definitely worth the effort involved. They further agree that the breadth and diversity of learning experiences excited and stimulated not only the students, but teachers and other parents as well. In addition, they found a successful program of parent participation requires teachers to carefully nurture and actively encourage parents.

Several years earlier, the research and experiences from working with schools and families nationally led Rich, Mattox, and Van Dien (1979) to believe that

1. Parent involvement with schools is successful only when its goal is increased student motivation and achievement.
2. The overwhelming majority of parents, regardless of their socioeconomic and educational backgrounds, possess the basic strengths and abilities to help their children achieve.

These three authors also believe, for the same reasons, that

1. Schools, no matter how understaffed or ill-equipped, have the capabilities of reaching out and effecting parental involvement, by using easy inexpensive materials.
2. Schools should start with what the family has instead of worrying about what it does not have.
3. Home environment, no matter how poor, is a citadel of care and concern for children; that is, family concern can be readily translated into practical support for children and schools. (Rich, Mattox and Van Dien, 1979, pp. 506–510).

These authors reiterate that professional educators have always known intuitively what research had revealed in earlier studies (Barth, 1978; Rich, 1976, 1977; Stanford Research Institute, 1983): that parents are the most important teachers of their children; that it is the parents, rather than the school, who are ultimately responsible for their children's education. Therefore, the much-touted concept that often becomes a stumbling block to progress may be redirected toward positive ends. In essence, the nondeficit model can be used to build on the existing strengths, ingenuity, and creativity of homes and schools without waiting for what would probably never come in the form of organizational change and massive public funding.

The fact is that parents are generally interested in ways that may help their own children; ways that are relatively easy, fast, and linked to their children's school environment.

In the traditional vein, parent-school communication usually comes in the form of report cards, conferences, and newsletters in order to keep parents informed. Most of this communication is initiated by the school and parents play relatively passive roles therein. Additionally, policy making usually takes the form of parent advisory committees. Relatively few parents can, or wish to, participate in such committees. To generate further and better interest, parents must feel wanted, trusted, and involved. And, certainly parental education is needed here (Bennett & Le Compte, 1990; Sobol, 1987; Trotter, 1987).

Parental education and training have helped parents not only work better with their children but also improve their own family life. Of all the models identified, parental education and meaningful involvement have been the most substantive. The home and the community become identified as vital influences, intimately linked with student success. In the process of upgrading or generally improving parental skills, teacher-helpers come to acknowledge that parents really care about their children and that they have the capacity to do what is right for their children, regardless of their economic and educational backgrounds.

In a very special way, a commitment to parental involvement may be enhanced if schools are able to apply the following recommendations as a way of mutually reinforcing the home-school efforts:

1. Schools must show a genuine desire to involve parents and not simply pay lip service to the concept of parental involvement.
2. Effective planning for parental involvement must include honest dialogue that allows parents to have significant input into how best to handle agendas, provide assistance, and identify needed staff.
3. A reciprocal or two-way outreach between the school and the community of parents must be created, with the community at large being a visible and viable partner as well.
4. Simultaneously, the school must serve both as a focal point for the repository of many community services and

activities, as well as the center of a massive, meaningful outreach base which funnels educational leadership and programmatic packages to off-site centers in other nearby locations within the community (National Committee for Citizens in Education, 1982, pp. 37–47).

In fulfilling these recommendations, the school will likely continue to dominate philosophical considerations in the foreseeable future as it dispenses its twofold purposes of the public school: transmitting the values of the society while producing a literate citizenry. In the final analysis, the importance of improving our schools cannot be underestimated, given the growing concern about the effects of education and the need to enact reform measures to help youngsters who are having difficulty at school. Measures that include adequate time and resources of educational goods and services are of paramount necessity, especially for helping "at-risk" students achieve success and in providing for special programmatic arrangements that will raise the performance of low-achieving students. It stands to reason that children who are designated as being at-risk are not properly educated; that is, if they fail to receive a "good" education and consequently "good" jobs, they suffer as individuals, but society at large will also suffer economic and social consequences. Hence, one major concern in this context is that parents should be given more assistance to help with their children's schooling and thus much more involvement in the tripartite sharing of responsibility with the school and its community in the education of their children. In essence, educational reform policies and administrative practices of enduring parental involvement can show advantages (Schaps & Solomon, 1990).

But parents need to extend themselves and further justify their inclusion in the responsible task of educating the nation's children and youth. Of significance here is that idea that they should assume the accompanying responsibilities that relate to education and schooling. They need to extend themselves by using their awareness for organizational efforts. Establishing networks of associations is a logical step (Getzels, 1978).

SCHOOLS, PARENTS, AND ASSOCIATIONS

In a majority of situations, parents are a child's first and most endearingly influential teachers. Therefore, success in a child's schooling must depend to some degree on the collaboration of home and school. Both institutions must work together for the commonweal or good of the child. In concert, when the school reflects the values of the home and the home correspondingly supports the efforts of the school, a child can grow in an atmosphere of shared purpose as well as consistent expectations (Sonnier, 1982; Walburg, 1984).

For these and other cogent reasons, parents or caregivers should remain active participants in their children's education throughout their school years. Of course, a reality is that there are quite often many barriers to such participation, especially in large urban environments. Besides, schools have, within the context of their traditional operation, barely defined limited and ancillary roles for parents. In addition, schools have, by reason of their structure and function, presented themselves as forbidding institutions which have held parents at bay. In such situations, parents have found it extremely difficult to work with teachers and administrators of their children's schools (Coleman, 1987; Rich, 1976, 1977).

The fact is that if children are to succeed with their schooling, home and school must share a harmony of mission; they must work together. It simply means that if parents are to become partners in their children's schooling, then schools must reach parents part of the way; they must reach out and involve parents. By the same token, parents need to take part in programs and decisions that would thereby enable them to participate in critical educational decision making that affects their children. In short, as partners in education, parents have certain rights and responsibilities. Some of these rights include the right to (1) know what is expected of the child; (2) know what and how the child is being taught; (3) know what programs the child is making on a timely basis; (4) be informed of the child's experiences and difficulties; (5) see the child's school records; (6) visit the child's school and talk to the child's teachers and principal; (7) be encouraged and assisted to participate in educational decision making; (8) be treated with courtesy and respect by school personnel.

Parents' responsibilities may include (1) sending the child to school rested, clean, fed, and ready to study and learn; (2) ensuring that the child attend school regularly; (3) maintaining continuous contact with the child's teachers and principal; (4) reinforcing at home the importance of acquiring knowledge, skills, and values that are needed to function in society; (5) volunteering time, skills, or resources when needed and possible; (6) taking part in school and community programs that empower parents to participate in making educational decisions; and (7) responding to communications from the child's school (New York State Education Department, 1991).

PARENT NETWORK

Besides the traditional Parent Teachers Association, various agencies and individuals have developed programs for parents. These are meant to serve for the promulgation of parents. Many of these include surveys, climate studies, evaluation by observation, and study councils. Basically, they are all parts of the dynamics of empowering parents, so that they can share in a most meaningful way in the decision-making process of issues affecting their own and other children's schooling, as part of a larger civic responsibility (Filipczak et al., 1977). In recent years, parents as citizens have become more active in shared decision making. This kind of involvement has assumed two dramatic postures. One involves school evaluation and the other involves the establishment of parent councils. In the case of evaluation, programs have been established for use by parents and other citizens. One very important organization is the National Committee for Citizens in Education (NCCE), a parent network that works to improve children's education. The following is a partial listing; additional information may be obtained by writing to the individual or agency that has developed the program.

- *Working With Your School.* Published by the Texas Advisory Committee on Civil Rights. Available at no charge from the U.S. Commission on Civil Rights, Publication Warehouse, 621 N. Payne Street, Alexandria, Virginia 22314. The publication contains an evaluation model which can be used by parents.
- *Evaluating the Educational Outcomes of Your Local School: A Manual for Parents and Citizens.* Published by the Citizens Research Council of Michigan, 500 Guardian Building, South, Detroit, Michigan 48226.
- *Schools Can Be Evaluated.* Published by School Management Study Group 440, East First Street South, Salt Lake City, Utah 84111.
- *A Procedure for Assessing the Performance of a Particular School.* Prepared by Michael Scriven for the San Francisco Public Schools Commission, Board of Education, San Francisco United School District, 135 Van Ness, San Francisco, California 94102.
- *The School Survey.* Published by the National Urban Coalition, 2100 M. Street NW, Washington, D.C. 20031.
- *School Climate Study.* Developed by Eugene Howard, Colorado Department of Education, 201 East Colfax Avenue, Denver, Colorado 80203.
- *Taking Stock of Your School Educational Leadership.* Published by the Association for Supervision and Curriculum Development, 225 N. Washington Street, Alexandria, Virginia 22314.
- *What Is a Survey?* Published by American Statistical Association, 806 Fifteenth Street NW, Washington, D.C. 20005.
- *Information for Parents on School Evaluation* (Educational Testing Service TM Report 421). Published by ERIC Clearinghouse on Tests, Measurement, and Evaluation (ED 0994 32). Available from ERIC Document Reproduction

Service, P.O. Box 190, Arlington, Virginia 22210. Contains a good list of additional references that can provide information to parents on how to evaluate schools.
- *Moving: A Guide to Selecting a School System.* Published by Pautler Associates, 50 Bragg Court, Amherst, New York 14221.
- *Community Opinion Survey.* Published by the Kenmore–Town of Tonawanda Public Schools, Kenmore, New York 1421J.
- *Parent Opinion Inventory.* Published by National Study of School Evaluation, 5201 Leesburg Pike, Falls Church, Virginia 22041.
- *How to Choose a School.* By Bruce Kemble. Express Newspapers, Ltd., Standard House, 56 Farrington Street, London, England EC4A 4DY.

In recent years, parents and citizens have become more active in school evaluation. Parents have formed such organizations as Parent Information Center in Teaneck, New Jersey, and the Parents Union for Public Schools in Philadelphia, Pennsylvania. They are indicative of the strong interest that parents have in their schools. Both are members of the Parents' Network of the NCCE. For assistance in forming a local parent association or to join the Parents' Network, write 410 Wilde Lake Village Green, Columbia, Maryland 21044; or call (301) 997-9300.

PARENT COUNCILS

Having parent advisory or governance councils at each school is an effective way of improving schools. Such councils help to solve problems, develop cooperative decision-making processes, and articulate school needs to the community. Councils can be of two kinds: advisory and governance. Advisory councils study situations and make recommendations. They may evaluate the school and make recommendations for improvement. The principal and the staff decide which recommendations will be implemented. In many places, advisory councils are not highly regarded by parents because they feel that the councils put a lot of energy into problem solving without having any power to make changes (Spring, 1991). Governance councils have more authority; they have an equal standing with school personnel. Such a relationship makes it possible for them to decide with equal voice which recommendations should be implemented. In some schools, this is called "shared governance." Under such cooperative governance, good things seem to happen: achievement improves, attendance increases, community support intensifies, and public confidence in the school increases. Some people refer to "shared governance" as the Japanese "quality circles" management system (National Committee for Citizens in Education, 1982).

REFERENCES

Appel, K. (1985). *America's changing families: A guide for educators.* Bloomington, Indiana. Phi Delta Kappa Educational Leadership, *52*(1), 52.

Banks, J. A. (1981). *Multiethnic education.* Boston: Allyn & Bacon.

Barth, R. (October, 1978). Parents as helpers, critics, and adversaries. *National Elementary Principal, 58*(1), 52.

Bennett, K. P. & Le Compte, M. D. (1990). *The way schools work.* New York: Longman.

Bennett, W. L. (1988). *American education: Making it work.* Washington, D.C.: Government Printing Office.

Bronfenbrenner, U. (1979). *The ecology of human development.* Cambridge, Massachusetts: Harvard University Press.

Cochran, M. (Fall, 1987). The parental empowerment process: Building on family strengths. *Equity and Choice, 4*(1), 9–22.

Coleman, J. (August–September, 1987). Families and schools. *Educational Leadership, 16,* 32–38.

Cremin, L. A. (1977). *Tradition of American education.* New York: Basic Books.

———. (May, 1978). Family-community linkages in American education: Some comments on the recent historiography. *Teachers College Record, 79,* 7.

Davies, D. (Fall, 1987). Looking for an ecological solution. *Equity and Choice* 4(1), 3–7.

Dewey, J. (1938). *Experience and education.* New York: Macmillan.

Evans, K. M. (1962). *Sociometry and education.* London: Routledge & Kegan Paul.

Filipczak, J. et al. (April 1977). *Parental involvement in the schools: Towards what ends?* Silver Springs, Maryland: Institute for Behavioral Research.

Getzels, J. W. (May, 1978). The communities of education. *Teachers College Record, 79*(4), 659–682.

Goetz, J. P. & Le Compte, M. D. (1984). *Ethnography and qualitative design in educational research.* Orlando, Florida: Academic Press.

Gough, P. B. (1989). Looking to the future. *Phi Delta Kappa* 70(9), 658.

Heath, S. B. (1981). *Ways with words: Language, life, and work in communities and classrooms.* New York: Cambridge.

Henderson, A. T. (Winter, 1988). Good news: An ecologically balanced approach to academic improvement. *Educational Leadership,* 66(2), 60–3.

Hobbs, N. (1978). Families, schools, and communities: An ecosystem for children. *Teachers College Record, 79,* 755–766.

[The] Home and School Institute. (1978–1979). *Families learning together.* Washington, D. C.: Home and School Institute.

Johnston, M. & Slotnik, J. (February, 1985). Parent participation in the schools: Are the benefits worth the burdens? *Phi Delta Kappa,* 66(6), 430–433.

Leitcher, H. J. (May, 1978). Families and communities as educators: Some concepts of relationships. *Teacher College Record,* 79(4), 567–659.

National Committee for Citizens in Education. (1982). *Your School: How well is it working?* Columbia, Maryland: NCCE.

National Governors' Association. (1986). *Time for results.* Task Force on Parent Involvement and Choice Report. Washington, D. C.: Government Printing Office.

New York State Education Department. (July, 1991). *A New Compact for Learning.* Albany, New York: State Education Department.

Parsons, T. (1959). The school's class as a social system: Some of its functions in American society. *Harvard Educational Review, 29,* 297-31g.

———. (1951). *The social system.* Glencoe, Illinois: Free Press.

Rich, D. (1977). *A family affair: Education.* Washington, D.C.: Home and School Institute.

———. (1976). *The relationship of the home learning laboratory technique to first grade student achievement.* Unpublished doctoral dissertation, Catholic University of America. Washington D.C.

Rich, D., Mattox, B. & Van Dien, J. (April, 1979). Building on family strengths: The non-deficit involvement model for teaming home and school. *Educational Leadership 36*(7), 506–510.

Schaps, E. & Solomon, D. (November, 1990). Schools and classrooms as caring communities. *Educational Leadership, 48*(3), 38–42.

Silber, J. (1989). *Straight schooling: What is wrong with American education and how to fix it.* New York: Harper and Row.

Sobol, T. (Nov. 15, 1987). The region extending the reach of schools: Down to infants, to parenting. *New York Times,* Section 4, p. 6.

Sonnier, I. L. (1982). Holistic education: How I do it. *College Student Journal, 16,* 64–67.

Spring, J. (1991). *American education: An introduction to social and political aspects.* White Plains, New York: Longman Publishing Group.

Stanford Research Institute. (1983). *Parent involvement in compensatory education programs.* Washington, D.C.: Office of Planning, Budgeting, and Evaluation.

Trotter, R. J. (September, 1987). Growth spirit mirror mental milestones. *Psychology Today, 21*(9), 13.

Ungar, M. S. (September, 1988). Beyond the cookies are carnivals. *School Administrators, 8*(45), 56.

Walburg, H. J. (1984). Improving the productivity of America's schools. *Educational Leadership, 41*, 19–27.

———. (1984). Families as partners in educational productivity. *Phi Delta Kappan, 65*(6), 397–400.

Weber, M. (1947). *The theory of social and economic organizations.* (Henderson, A.M. and Parsons, T., Translators). New York: Oxford University Press.

Weiler, K. (1988). *Women teaching for change.* South Hadley, Massachusetts: Beger and Garvey.

Chapter 6

EMPOWERMENT FOR ALL PARENTS

The tendency of people to rationalize their manifestations takes the burden off deep-seated, underlying problems. If they admit that the needs are real, that they exist and are the sources of the many discrepancies, then they would have to acknowledge that something is wrong, to identify what is wrong, and to work honestly and assiduously to rectify what is wrong. This would imply removing the impediments that create limited educational opportunities, a sobriquet which is an artificial category that separates groups of people without legitimate bases.

Within the context of such circumstances, there is a need to understand differences between schooling, which is rooted in institutional bureaucratic and ritualistic behavior, and learning, which is fundamentally a developmental and introspective activity. Unfortunately, the connection between schooling and learning is often troublingly blurred or severed. To rectify this would require new organization, conceptualization, attitudes, materials, and tools that would enable learners to go easily beyond the information given in traditional school settings; to forge new connections and understandings from delivered information, and to represent and communicate imaginative constructions with scope for change (Gifford, 1990).

PEDAGOGY OF PARTICIPATION

But legitimate as these concerns are or seem to be, it must be also considered that no understanding of our times is complete without a vision of the relationship between education and schooling and, by implication and actuality, the relationship between education and schooling and the larger society; between and among the influencers and the influences of the larger ecological environment, including the school as an institution. The fact is that knowledge has assumed such criticality as a factor of production that schools can no longer be considered mere instruments of socialization. Instead, today, schools powerfully shape, limit, and interpret general participation in the dynamic human drama which transcends the socialization process.

According to Cross (1974), like most social inventions, schooling evolves faster than our understanding of its implications. Periodically, we struggle to catch up, trying to muster enough understanding to wrestle as equals with history. Accordingly, we consciously shape the institutions that shape us. There is a reciprocity here, which provides an exciting encounter as new visions of schooling hold us up to our faith and our choices. But, just as school is expected to provide the specially crafted experiences, the efficaciousness of offerings that are available at other institutions, it is prudent to consider the potency of assistance that other complementary or support services may provide. Parent participation in the dynamic power of schooling can do just that: strengthen schooling and expand its civilizing mission.

Today, many educational issues confront the nation. But in spite of the continuing discourse about parental participation, school people generally feel that parents as a whole are not usually savvy enough to assume leadership roles in schools; that is, their presence in classrooms is sometimes seen as an encroachment, a matter that impinges on territoriality. In schools, there is the tendency to think of family and parental involvement as occurring on the school's turf, and there is the assumption that poor parental attendance at school events means that parents are not involved because they do not care. The truth is that parents must, and often, wish to be active participants in their children's schooling. Most parents consider the welfare of their children a key concern. They want to be seen as more than bystanders in the educational process; that is, not only as someone to see that homework is done or to chaperone class trips. In fact, parents wish to exercise the fundamental right to know, to understand, and to share in decisions that affect the education of their children; they need to be informed about teachers and principals, about the curriculum, and about school policies (Rowell, 1981).

There is a sense that parents would like to acquire some control over their children's education, to see themselves as being effective, both intellectually and emotionally. This implies exercising their influence as broadly as possible to include such functions as audience, teachers-at-home, volunteers, paid employees, and decision makers (Gordon & Breivogel, 1976). Parents seek to establish a partnership, a common effort toward common goals, a necessity (Seeley, 1982) which may serve to counteract inhibitions (Henderson, 1989).

But barriers do exist in many parent-school relationships. Some of these barriers are inadvertently erected by schools themselves. Wilson, Pentecoste, and Nelms (1983), in their study on the effects of age, race, occupation, and education on parents' communication with schools, conclude that one of the educational problems that has been widely published in the press and articulated by parent groups has been the difficulty of communicating with the school. Parents, for example, appear to believe that grade school educational institutions are both dogmatic and authoritarian (Cronin & Hailer, 1973). School personnel have been viewed by parents as specialized experts who bully them with their expertise (Doebla, 1971).

Wilkerson (1970) asserted that economically poor parents are usually made to feel quite uncomfortable when they visit schools by officious and paternalizing school personnel.

Ryan (1976), on the other hand, has argued that parents are generally uncomfortable in school situations even though they are supportive and anxious about their children's progress. Teachers, Ryan continues, are uncomfortable about discussing children with parents and tend to reject any information that might sound like advice because of the possibility that it might reflect on their professional competence. In fact, the problems of parent-school communication are as important as they are complicated. For these and other reasons, the perception of school-community communication by parents is an important factor susceptible to many influences.

Therefore, in addition to examining these barriers, school can and must build strong family involvement programs that can validate and encourage a parental and family involvement that supports children's education, both at home and at school. If schools treat parents as unimportant negative influences on their children's school or if they discourage parents from becoming involved, then they promote the development of the attitudes that inhibit achievement at school (Henderson, 1989).

Instead of making the parents' involvement in the school's function marginal, it is prudent that parents be encouraged to become educational decision makers in the shared governance of schools. They should be convinced that they are needed, that teachers and other school people value their input, and that school people are willing to listen to and work with them without being threatening and manipulative. In general, there is a need for shared accountability such that teachers may feel relieved of the burden of being assigned a disproportionate amount of the responsibility for child rearing, because parents have more influence and responsibility for their children; that they should receive help in improving themselves as parents; and, that shared participation and true decision making find support in school programs which focus on both parent and child development (Strom, 1984). Such dramatic but inevitable changes can certainly create a shift from communicating information to parents to communicating with parents (Stafford, 1987).

There is an element of irony surrounding the inclusion of parents in public school involvement and decision making. Although this custom of parent participation is rooted in U.S. educational history, the fact is that while middle- and upper-income parents have had easy access to teachers and administrators, as well as explicit means of participation, low-income, less advantaged parents have traditionally been unable to use these same modes of participation (Pysykowski, 1989). This is even more so for African-American, Hispanic, and Asian parents. Involvement is linked with parity, which these groups do not necessarily have.

Over time, discourse about the policy of parental involvement has been centered around three questions: (1) Does parental involvement work? (2) Should it be a policy or priority? (3) Is it feasible as a target for policy? (Melargno, et al., 1981). Indeed, these apprehensions accompanying the issue of parental participation are both implied and expressed. Here, the issue of parity of participation becomes questionable only when parents are of low-income status and dwell in inner city or large urban environments. Thus, the general conclusion is that most strategies for parental involvement have not been carried out as they were originally intended. Meanwhile, efforts to stimulate parental participation have remained largely uneven, especially in urban schools. This persistent problem adversely affects public education and often undermines many otherwise good intentions.

Altogether, these assumptions about parental participation—empowerment, if you will—have, at best, spawned limited, isolated, but meaningful successes and a healthy discourse on the subject with much of the focus, at least for now, appearing to be mired at the ideational level of chalk and talk. Thus, while the term "empowerment" carries the democratic ring of political expediency and certainly the promise of good prospects for educational application, many powerful decision makers in the larger ecological environment remain quite skeptical.

In light of these factors, educating the public about the possibilities of true parental empowerment, especially in a climate of critical educational change, remains essential, not only for the purpose of general orientation, but also for the obvious need to help shape public sentiments that the main concern for parents is not parity, but rather, better education for their children. In a more profound sense, these issues call into question the political reality of empowerment and the related factor of rights and responsibilities, basic ingredients of the philosophical concerns of freedom, liberty, and justice, the significance of which comes from actualization.

WHAT IS EMPOWERMENT?

Empowerment suggests a process by which people become better able to influence those persons and organizations that affect their lives or those they care about (Vanderslice, 1984). Empowerment is also linked to helping persons to remove obstacles that impede efforts to achieve status within a broad social structure. Accordingly, educational empowerment appears to be a logical requirement for all parties, meaning: individuals, groups, institutions, agencies that are somehow involved in the process of educating children. In particular, therefore, parents require many, as well as varied, types of resources that would enable them to provide the at-home support for children as students.

But whether empowerment implies changing teacher attitudes to overcome their devaluing of working-class families in the final analysis, empowerment should involve planning new, positive relations between and among parents, the school, and its community. It should also mean promoting initiatives within the school's community; that is, among local authorities, individuals, groups, agencies, and other institutions that support the education of children and youth. As well, it should mean expending energy and effort in the establishment of better connections among the different aspects of the children's lifespaces.

It stands to reason that if all personalities, individual participants, and institutions exercised their political will and imagination in really addressing the prevailing educational problems, substantial benefits may be derived for the children's development and, thus, for school success; for parents; for teachers and schools; for communities; and for the advancement of a more just and democratic society (Chavkin, 1989).

PARENTAL INVOLVEMENT IN EDUCATION

For a variety of reasons, parental apathy has remained a somewhat recurring theme among issues surrounding the delivery of urban educational goods and services. In some instances, the causes are found outside of the policies and practices; as well, teacher attitude may be part of the problem; so is a lack of sensitivity, an ingredient that is so essential for overcoming cultural and social class barriers. A pertinent question here asks about the matter of apathy and the impediments that generate it. To address these impediments which restrict participation, there ought to be new postures that transcend mere talk and chalk.

First, parental involvement must be seen from the standpoint of its positivistic possibilities. For instance, parental involvement in education can contribute to the empowerment of parents themselves, as well as their motivation to participate eventually, in larger societal interests and activities. Through empowerment, parents can constitute themselves as power groups, for example, which can influence educational policy that often advances the democratization of educational equity and quality. But parental empowerment is usually predicated on people's initial involvement, which is tied to their self-worth, and to their adequacy and motivation to initiate their own involvement to strengthen their own networks, and to decide about the resumption of their own education and advancements. In essence, parents must receive the necessary cooperation and assistance which is critical to their effectiveness.

HELPING PARENTS PREPARE

Despite the wide variety of choices offered in our society, everything from politics to religion, cars to breakfast cereals, there are piteously few significant choices within public school systems for parental participation. With public schools controlling both the production and consumption of education, students and their parents, especially in low-income, urban districts, have very little to say about these important matters. However, a reasonable belief still exists that the two publics, the school and its consumers, can work toward the elevation of the sovereignty of a sound, ethical, and philosophical purpose.

This lack of choice has helped to create a passive attitude among many parents. Thus, some parents are not significantly involved in their children's education, at least not in the way they would prefer. It is therefore imperative that change should be brought about so that, through working more closely with schools, parents are given scope to become involved in their children's education. Perhaps, in so doing, they may be able to provide what the "experts" have so far been unable to accomplish. In essence, what parents need at this point in educational history, more than ever, include procedures of assistance that may come through training in skills and techniques which they can apply at the level of the "teaching home" as they grapple with the responsibility of helping with their children's education, especially in a climate of crisis.

Whatever must be done, in terms of helping parents become significant participants in the function of their children's school, should begin with a sense of promoting a culture of concern. Such a concern must seek its underpinnings in the creation of greater awareness and sensitivity toward overt parental desire for involvement and should include the following:

1. Carefully planned activities involving people who work together. Such activities should be developed to draw attention to parental involvement, through programs that require wider recognition.
2. Outstanding parent involvement which should be organized, showcased, and rewarded. The product outcome of these efforts should receive the cooperation of the state department, which, in turn, should work with professional organizations of educators, administrators, and local school board members to disseminate successful product outcomes and, thereby publicize vital award-winning programs.
3. The creation of a statewide task force to address further parental and community involvement in order to identify outstanding programs and, consequently, to make recommendations to policy makers, business people in the private and public sectors, educators, and community groups.
4. Annual conferences on the theme of parental and community involvement in education. Invited participants should include parents, educators, and business and community groups.

Another issue in the plethora of activities to be provided in support of parents should include the provision of technical assistance. Such assistance should be given to school districts with amenities to be made available for parental training in skills and strategies for improving participation. Thus, in collaboration with local school authorities, and beginning at the state level, such education departments should work quite closely with school districts, intermediate units, and such professional and community organizations as parent associations, as well as home and school institutes, all working in cooperation with universities and colleges, to help develop and refine parental training. There should also be competitive demonstration grant programs which may be offered to school districts that are willing, ready, and able to experiment with schoolwide management programs. In addition, all school districts within states should be eligible for such grants, which should cover, among other things, planning and training activities. Finally, in the case of small, urban and rural school districts, which lack resources for placing needed challenging and supportive programs, states should help by providing funds to such districts or schools, in order to establish needed training programs for parents.

Since increased parental involvement requires the development of specific skills, state authorities must help parental involvement in public school education, generating and making available assistance to school districts that are to experiment and share their findings with other schools. In addition, prospective teachers and administrators should receive specific and related instruction regarding how they should hold parent conferences and show parents ways to reinforce and extend classroom lessons at home thereby involving parents in advisory as well as school-site management committees.

PARENTAL RESPONSIBILITIES

Whereas many of the above suggestions may prove to be very helpful for many parents, conventional wisdom suggests that the working parent requires special considerations. Because of sociopolitical and economic circumstances, this new constituency of parents has become a very viable contingency in the kaleidoscopic landscape. In many ways, it is this category of parents that often distances itself from the school and its activities, largely because of the constraints of having to work. This new phenomenon on the economic horizon adds to an already, seemingly disenchanted group of parents.

It has become an accepted fact, for instance, that many working parents may be well-intentioned in their purpose, and would really appreciate keeping the parent-school relationships intact, but the added difficulty of coping with the rigors of work and those associated with maintaining a family often place overwhelming restrictions on their efforts toward participation. This is in addition to factors described previously. It is a reality that truly warrants recognition and consideration in the educational scheme of things. It does not necessarily mean that parents so circumstanced are uninterested in school involvement, their children's education, or participation in the decision-making processes of schools. Quite the contrary!

At any rate, working parents can and should stay in touch with their children's school, as well as the school-related and supportive services of their community. This act of keeping in touch is a significant part of parenting, of sustaining the family. Of course, staying in touch may assume a variety of forms. Little acts, such as putting a note in a child's lunchbox, a reader, or a pocket of the school bag, or simply taping a special message on the child's tape recorder, calculator, or favorite coloring book will, in all likelihood, be reflected in the child's character later on. Such gestures help parents to sustain their gut interests.

Two issues are implicit there. First is the issue of the parents having an obligation to themselves and another to the child. But, overall, parental help must receive specific and significant attention if the parents are expected to make the helping overtures on behalf of the child. Educating parents, then, becomes a crucial consideration. They must be diligently encouraged, helped, and given the kind of assistance and support that suggests they are wanted in the schools, that their presence and function are appreciated.

PARENT EDUCATION

Although many parents may lack knowledge, they often do not necessarily lack interest in the schools their children attend. Parent-school partnerships which have typically defined the content, structure, and scheduling of parental involvement activities on the school's terms must, to truly service parents, be done with, by, and for parents themselves. The fact is that parental involvement works, and there is much proof that this is really so. Efforts to stimulate parental participation, however, must be even. Significant incorporation of parental participatory involvement requires two essential ingredients. First, there must be a belief in the ability of parents to contribute in important ways to the education of their children. Second, there must be willingness to make an effort to involve all parents, including low-income parents, in that special enterprise of school decision making. Where these essentials are missing, parental education becomes a much needed factor. For these reasons, the following considerations should underscore efforts to provide parental education:

1. Parental education should integrate both cognitive and effective principles, methods, and procedures. It should also help create an awareness of skills, attitudes, and understandings which may enable parents to become more effective as partners in their children's education.
2. The establishment of comprehensive planning institutes should bring together parents; various experts in the fields of education, social, and psychological services; as well as staffers of school-improvement committees. These groups can plan cogent proposals for introducing curricular change; for establishing discipline codes; and for placing agreement on the needs of particular schools, especially as they relate to basic facts on after-school issues, such as homework and the like.

3. Participation in the conceptualization and development of a parenting program must utilize local resources in conjunction with issues and ideas of the experts, for a comprehensive program of hope and reality, undergirded by theory and practice.
4. Parents functioning as teachers should receive specific suggestions for helping their children in the home-school setting; and, these specifics should include classwork in helping strategies, as well as skills and techniques of study plans and their proper execution.
5. Wherever it is found that assumptions about the ability of parents to offer assistance to their children are faulty, opportunities should be created so that needs may be satisfied, doubts removed, and required skills sharpened, established, and upgraded.
6. In collaboration, the successes, whatever they are and however minimal, should be celebrated with all of schools' participants and community liaisons and well-wishers. At such happenings, efforts should be made to publicize what exists and is working, as well as to dramatize the need for more participants as facilitators for improved school and home interaction.

Finally, in all activities, students should be vitally involved when parents are successful. Children should help share the successes and their messages, and they should celebrate the cogent efforts as they pass the word about their parents and the schools' successes.

Parents are their children's first and, in many instances, most influential teachers. The home efforts can therefore greatly improve student achievement. However, when parents find themselves in vulnerable positions or with handicapping conditions, they should certainly be helped, so that they may be able to meet the challenge of providing the extension services to their children at home where, away from their teachers and other immediate school personnel, they require support, such as encouragement, assurance, understanding, empathy, and know-how, particularly when they engage in the critical assignments brought to the teaching-home, such as homework.

In the years ahead, parental participation in school affairs shall become increasingly more effective. Among other educational movements, parental activism, despite current opposition, will produce a most dramatic change in the governance of schools. Parents will eventually become equal partners with professionals regarding what schools can and cannot do. Also, they will become equally responsible for the success or failure of U.S. public education, because the truth is that schools cannot succeed without parental participation and support.

The movement to intensify parent involvement in school affairs began in the mid-1970s. In effect, it has already received impetus across the nation by the National Committee for Citizens in Education (NCCE), the School Management Study Groups (SMSG), and the Institute for Responsive Education (IRE). These three organizations urge parents to become active participants in school decision making, in recognition of parents' rights and in building partnerships between homes and schools.

Essentially they function as enablers for parents to acquire and retain confidence in the schools, while serving to promulgate competence in the education of all children: black, brown, and white. They operate on the assumption that parental activism will benefit the schools; they urge too, that schools need to respond to parental movements. They suggest that principals need to develop new skills much the same as teachers, since both groups will need to understand the new concept of shared governance in education. For just as some school people may become defensive and frightened by parental power, some parents may exercise their newly found influence irresponsibly.

Just the same, there must be compromises, so that when the anxiety subsides and there is then a meeting of the minds of the various publics and constituencies, a new coalition will have been forged and stronger and more efficient schools will have been established. This is critical.

Partnerships with parents will increase support, infuse the schools with important ideas, and make parents accountable for helping the schools execute their numerous and varied jobs. While in the initial stages the issues are ones of parental rights, in the final analysis, parental participation, activism, and collaboration are all matters of responsible action, of the democratic process being actualized. When this happens as it ought to, across the nation, the nation's schools will have been placed in good hands.

REFERENCES

Chavkin, N. F. (1989). A multicultural perspective on parent involvement: Implications of policy and practice. *Education, 109*, 276–285.

Cronin, J. & Hailer, R. (1973). *Organizing an urban school system for diversity*. Lexington, Massachusetts: Lexington Books.

Cross, D. (December, 1974). Pedagogy of participation. *Teachers College Record, 76*(2), 314–334.

Doebla, C. H. (1971). *Planning your child's education*. Englewood Cliffs, New Jersey: Prentice-Hall.

Gifford, B. (June, 1990). Education on my mind. *Education Week, IX*(39), 9.

Gordon, I. J. & Breivogel, W. F. (1976). *Building effective home-school relationships*. Boston: Allyn and Bacon.

Henderson, A. T. (1989). Parents: School's best friends. *Phi Delta Kappan, 70*, 148–153.

Melargno, R. et al. (1981). *Parents and the federal education programs*. Santa Monica, California: Systems Development Corp.

Pysykowski, I. S. (1989). Parents as partners in educating the young. *Education, 109*, 286–294.

Rowell, J. C. (1981). The five rights of parents. *Phi Delta Kappan, 65*, 441–443.

Ryan, C. (1976). *The open partnerships equality in running the schools*. New York: McGraw-Hill.

Seeley, D. S. (November, 1982). Education through partnership. *Educational Leadership*, 42–43.

Stafford, L. (1987). Parent-teacher communication. *Communication Education, 36*, 182–187.

Strom, R. D. (1984). The home-school partnership: Learning to share accountability. *Clearing House, 57*, 315–317.

Vanderslice, V. (1984). Empowerment: A definition. *Human Ecology, 14*(1), 106–114.

Wilkerson, D. A. (1970). The failure of schools serving the black and Puerto Rican poor. In Rubenstein, A. T., (Ed.), *Schools against children* (pp. 93–126). New York: Monthly Press Review.

Wilson, J., Pentecoste, J. & Nelms, C. (1983). The effects of age, occupation, race, and education on parent communication with the schools. *Education, 103*(4), 402–404.

Chapter 7
REQUIRED: A POSITIVE SELF-CONCEPT

All societies which have persisted and flourished have traditionally made great efforts to ensure that children and youth, representatives of the future, support their central values. In Western democracies, particularly the United States, support for these cherished values is considered best achieved by maintaining an informed and literate citizenry.

In the course of a lifetime, people are usually faced with an incredible number and variety of decisions regarding phenomena, problems, and processes of group governance. These decisions often include selecting leaders; deciding how to manage conflicts or disagreements; choosing ways to handle the effects of intra- and interdependence; defining what rules to make or what goals to set. In practical terms, life demands of each individual the necessity to make tough decisions; ignoring the process does not make critical issues disappear.

At home or within a family, a person is faced with decisions about living most amicably with those close at hand. At work, for instance, or at school, decisions may concern: What needs to be done? With whom? For what ends? Similarly, persons are faced with decisions relative to their own community or outreach: How to respond to injustice or to illness? How to respond to the immediate needs of a neighborhood, the ecosystem, or other parts of the world and its human family? Or, it may just simply be to answer the question: What technical or academic school or college should one attend? More fundamentally, it may be: Just who am I, and how do I fit into the human family of planet earth? All of these concerns and issues demand responses. For unprepared, young adults, however, because of a variety of very telling circumstances, there is often the feeling of powerlessness that comes from their inability to cope with or to take charge of their lives, by making satisfying decisions regarding matters that touch them personally. Independent research studies (Gibb, 1964; Glasser, 1985; Howe & Howe, 1975; Lippett & Schindler-Raiman, 1973; Schutz, 1960; Weinstein and Fantini, 1970) indicate findings confirming that "control over one's life" is a universal human concern.

In general, adults and students need to understand the dynamics of what is going on around them, to look at responsible behavior, for example, and to understand how their learning situation meshes with the rest of society, as well as with the realities of their lives in school, home, family, community, the nation, and the world. In essence, all lives are full of ambiguities and rapid changes which require of everyone to make quick decisions often based on immediate available information. The need to make decisions is ever present.

Decision making may be defined as making reasoned choices among several alternatives. Reasoned choices are based on judgment which is consistent with the decision maker's values. They are also choices which are based on sound relevant information. Wise decision making involves skills of information-gathering and sifting; it involves too, skills in finding and evaluating information critical to the decisions to be made. Decision making means being able to know and deal with problems of uncertainty that are generated by the impossibility of uncovering all knowledge considered necessary to a decision. A common characteristic of all instances of logical decision making, whether they are personal or public decisions, is the existence of alternative

Required: A Positive Self-Concept

courses of action which requires judgment in terms of one's values. The development of decision making as a legitimate educational concern derives its justification from two basic value assumptions which underlie sociopolitical life. One is the belief in popular rule; the other is respect for the individual. From the democratic value of popular rule comes support for developing skills in making decisions about public issues. From the value of individual dignity comes the support for making sound decisions about personal problems. Individual dignity means respect for oneself as a person of worth and respect for others as well (Dewey, 1915).

But more than these factors is the understanding that making decisions requires the integration of cognitive and affective dynamics. Learning to make humane and socially affective decisions brings together and applies knowledge and understanding, as well as intellectual and interpersonal skills and values. The professional, pedagogical, and epistemological community must see the function of decision making as a process of preparing citizens who will approach issues with open minds and who will take positions that are based on logic, facts, reasoning, and careful analysis of all points of view (Cooley, 1964; Dewey, 1916).

If children, youth, and young adults are expected to become members of an able, literate citizenry with needed skills to make just and equitable social, political, and economic decisions or to delegate entities and individuals through legal and constitutional channels to do so for them, then critical thinking, logical problem-solving, and planned decision making skills on which these choices depend should be nurtured, emphasized, and not left to chance. If these learnings are to be achieved by a rational process, then settings must be organized, and cogent curricular and instructional practices should be developed, taught, and analyzed. Contexts must be created in which students have the opportunity to pose questions that require the establishment of alternative solutions and then to critically analyze them. Analysis is of paramount importance here; not just the exercise of compiling data. Therefore, to the extent that students are provided with decision-making skills, they can be nurtured or helped to fulfill individual potential and build self-esteem on which healthy, positive self-concepts may be crafted, as they filter into the larger ecological environment, equipped with skills that are necessary to support themselves and their dependents for self-actualization (Maslow, 1954) and society's commonweal or good (Dewey, 1902).

STUDENTS IN THE SOCIAL CONTEXT

Orienting a student toward a positive self-concept is an awesome undertaking that has its genesis in the ecosystem, beginning with the family and later finding complementarity in the school and its community. It is from the effects of the plethora of publics—the unique network of support systems within a child's ecosystem—that nurturance, enculturation, or political socialization derive their initial impetus. These special institutions or agencies (the family-home, community, and school) touch the life of children in a variety of ways and, therefore, play important roles in their education. Altogether, they affect the total lifespace of an individual child and thus help in establishing his or her individuality. We may say that these institutions or agencies collaborate or join together in influencing, facilitating, or helping a child's perception, behavior, or performance at school and elsewhere (Dewey, 1916).

In the home, there is that family which may consist of parents or caregivers, siblings, and sometimes other immediate relatives, such as grandparents, uncles, aunts, nieces, nephews, or cousins. In the community, there may be found other relatives, friends, neighbors, peers, and significant others who perhaps belong to other lay and religious groups. In the school, there are to be found a principal, teachers, and other personnel, such as a nurse, doctor, psychologist, psychiatrist, custodial engineer, guidance counselor, and guards. They are all part of the mechanism of modern-day schools, especially in large urban centers.

People are generally known to treasure the web of social relationships found in their neighborhoods because these relationships usually meet their needs for human contact and interaction. These social networks can also be instrumental in helping residents deal with some of life's problems. The help received from family, relatives, and neighbors, through formal and informal networks, are often well suited for providing, among other things, concrete advice, emotional reassurance, emergency help, long-term caring, and everyday assistance (Hallman, 1984). Moreover, attachment to place of residence is influenced by the social fabric of the neighborhood, such that a sense of community is most significant where residents have the strongest communal bonds. Also, such places are of greater racial homogeneity in which interaction among residents is shown to be highest (Ahlbrandt, 1984).

Altogether, the confluence of all of these agencies, services, and networks must generate and nurture a spirit or attitude which develops from within and serves as a driving force that governs beliefs and behaviors. It is the combined reflections of these beliefs, attitudes, and behaviors which then serve to characterize the fate of a people, a nation, that is then determined by the values which govern their decisions. These values may then be seen as: a love of truth; a sense of justice; a sense of personal responsibility; a spirit of cooperation; and a serving of the common good.

But like the student, a school must be ready to receive its charge. First, a school must reflect an embodiment of its goals. This should imply a demonstration/development of a positive sense of self and community, as well as a conscious effort at improving learning and student achievement (Rothman, 1991). The school should set leadership pace, focussing the school community on improving every aspect of itself, through the crucial element of total involvement of its teachers, parents, students, as well as administrators in educational decisions. More specifically, by seeking to improve the educational process by concentrating on curriculum and instruction undergirded by sound preparation, relevant content, and flexible pedagogy, it would encourage academic excellence.

SENSITIVITY

The type of school readiness that is discussed here moves the demand into the area of sensitivity respecting the school and its services. Implicitly, this means giving credence to such specific factors as:

- Teacher attitude toward students;
- A sense of commitment to the values, worth, and dignity of every child;
- Teacher behavior (e.g., how feelings, beliefs, and attitudes are acted out and the moral obligations that set the tone which students may emulate, as well as feel comfortable to study with);
- Teacher sensitivity to the fact that while students may differ ethnically or racially, they have similar educational needs which must be met;
- Sensitivity toward and willingness to meet the need for a heightened awareness in seeing human differences as natural, desirable, and beautiful;
- Demonstration of a rational reaction to any tendency or reference to stereotyping in classrooms or elsewhere in the school;
- A sensitivity toward assisting the movement of students from a narrow parochial attitude of ethnocentrisms toward a world view that recognizes and accepts the worth, dignity, and value of others;
- A sensitivity toward emotional, physical, and mental needs: to a knowledge of a student's environment and the social

forces which impinge upon the individual so circumstanced; and
- Teacher awareness of the meaning implied in the tone of the voice and its effect on students in terms of acceptance or rejection in classrooms and the school itself.

In essence, the demand for sensitivity which a school must exercise as part of its readiness status for the entering child clearly suggests the incorporation of innovative procedures that speak to current realistic and cogent needs. The use of functional pedagogy assumes special consideration here, as the school assumes and transacts the responsibility of placing those strategies that would nurture or facilitate reasonable human and academic growth.

One such strategy may be the application of situational teaching which has been promulgated by Scobie (1983). The concept of situational teaching refers to and focuses on the relationship between student achievement and self-direction in academic tasks. It underscores the effects which contingencies have on teaching. In this instance, aspects of the situation—student's level of self-direction, the classroom context and, the objectives to be achieved—are critical issues. Situational teaching underscores the significance of the efficaciousness of a school's personnel, in particular, its teachers who create conditions for students whose education should include helping them to confront choices while making meaningful decisions in a technological society; in not necessarily placing emphasis on what students can do, but rather, on what the teachers have enabled them to do, including individual and collaborative efforts (Brophy, 1979; Gibbons & Phillips, 1978; Glaser, 1977; Mischel, 1973; Schmuck & Schmuck, 1975). This is critical, as the degrees of freedom which teachers allow students, as well as the risks of innovation and practical departure from the ineffectual, become issues in the context of educational change.

SELF-ESTEEM

It follows, therefore, that by the time a child enters school, she or he should find an institution that is ready for carrying out the teaching-learning transaction, as a mandate, with efficiency. Given the nature of the child's ecosystem, it is reasonable to assume that the child has already formed a concept of self, whatever this is. That is, many ideas about the self and the results of interactions with significant others are already emplaced and at work. For the preschool child, the significant others will be primarily the child's mother, father, siblings, and possibly babysitters or nannies. Depending also on the child's background, there may be other significant people in his or her life.

A child's interaction with these significant people will form the basis for self-esteem. Self-esteem has two interrelated aspects. It entails a sense of personal efficacy and a sense of personal worth. It is the integrated sum of self-confidence and self-respect (Battle, 1982). Branden (1969) believes that individuals with high self-esteem tend to be more effective in meeting environmental demands than those persons with low self-esteem.

Self-esteem is constantly being reevaluated on the basis of new encounters or experiences. Therefore, as a child enters school, she or he will engage in many new interactions that will either enhance or lower his or her self-esteem. And since high self-esteem is positively correlated with being able to successfully meet the demands that life imposes, it stands to reason that educational systems should promote self-esteem in children (Ginot, 1972; Gordon, 1975).

Therefore, when a child enters school, it is also necessary to differentiate between global self-esteem and academic self-esteem. Global self-steem, according to Samuels (1977), refers to a child's general perception about himself or herself, whereas academic self-esteem refers to a child's perception regarding schoolwork. A student, for example, may have high self-esteem in one area but low self-esteem in another. Hence, before anything substantive may be done to improve self-esteem in students, it is important to understand what influences affect self-esteem in the first place (Briles, 1990). For example, in general, the following factors are said to have significant effects on self-esteem: (1) the amount of respectful, accepting, and concerned treatment received from significant others; (2) the history of successes and status, as well as positions held by persons in the individual's ecosystem and world; (3) the interpretation and modification of experiences that accord with values and aspiration; and (4) the individual's manner of responding to devaluation (Samuels, 1977, p. 34). These factors can be applied to the educational setting where a teacher becomes a significant other in a child's lifespace, in terms of the classroom climate, teacher attitude, instruction, assessment, grades, and awards (Hoge, Smith & Hanson, 1990). Thus, how a student performs at school may, indeed, become a condition of several factors, not the least of which is the nearest significant other, the teacher.

STUDENT PERFORMANCE

Once at school, the encounter of teachers and students is coordinated and played out in the teaching-learning transaction. These encounters, these experiences, are therefore, critical. The process becomes one of behavior modification (McDaniel, 1987); for indeed, education may be perceived as a change in behavior: a moving of the individual through flexibility, growth, and challenge from one level of development to another. How this process is managed becomes quite important. A basic interest of a child under such circumstances is to maintain and enhance self. But the success of this interest is as much a teacher responsibility as that of a student. How does this come about? What positive features should teachers pursue? From a values standpoint, there is always a tendency for persons to move towards that which they think is important and away from that which they feel is trivial or inconsequential. Excitement and challenge become added components here, as one considers the growing heterogeneity of classrooms in the nation that is largely urban.

Jacobson and Rosenthal (1968), through their research, demonstrated that attention fuels performance. It therefore follows that enthusiasm, expectation, and challenge will motivate students to perform better; that is, that positive expectations, attitudes, and responses will influence students' reaction and general classroom behavior. Similarly, the negative sides to these teacher demonstrations affect responses of disbelief in students' ability to perform. In essence, a teacher can become very instrumental in influencing a student's self-fulfilling prophecy. But teachers would be challenged to address their own needs, assumptions, and preparation, as well as those of their students. As decision makers who are constantly called on to think on their feet, teachers must also question themselves, their values, cognition and teaching styles, preparedness and openness to truth, revised truths, and suspended judgments (Jersild, 1952, 1955).

Teachers may question whether they can make a decision that is not popular, or can humanely live with one that their class as a group made as the best possible one. They may also question whether they trust others and, in return, are trusted; whether they like taking risks, can communicate effectively and can afford the time to lead, can stand the loneliness of leadership and live with the mistakes; whether they can admit being wrong, avoid making decisions, generate alternatives, and know how to compromise through negotiations. But, in addition to these concerns, the issue of interpersonal relationships soars high among priorities in classrooms where there is the need to help each other with school issues; make decisions in reference to problems; deal with anxieties, insecurities, and emotions that interfere with

Required: A Positive Self-Concept

reality, confidence, teaching, and learning (Bloom, 1982; Evans, 1962).

How, for instance, would teachers handle the mundane issue of complimenting students, especially those with poor images, and who require any and every opportunity which the warmth of a classroom may provide. Compare the following two models of compliments that are supposed to be issued by teachers, and try to flesh out the mental responses of students to whom these remarks, however well-intentioned, may have been directed:

Model A

1. You may be the leader today.

2. You have been such nice workers.

3. I could not have done it better myself.

4. I like the way you are working.

5. I like that; it has been well thought out.

Model B

1. You have a good head on today.

2. Look at who is right today.

3. You are one hundred percent correct.

4. Well, I should say you are using your head.

5. You are finally getting sharp today.

It may be clear here that implicit in these remarks is the issue of labelling, which often derives its sustenance from stereotyping. Teachers must be careful with language usage in the classroom. Students' sensitivity to remarks often survives long after passing references made by teachers. Some remarks may well have deleterious effects, going well beyond the immediacy of classroom years. For example, note the following instances in which persons are similarly circumstanced but differ in status and this difference is reflected in language:

1. If an adult seeks help, such gesture is often referred to as *consulting*, whereas if a child seeks help it is often referred to as *whining*.
2. If an adult is not paying attention to what is going on, it may be called *preoccupation*, but if a child is not listening it is usually referred to as *distractibility*.
3. If an adult forgets something, it may be called *absent-mindedness*, whereas if a child forgets something, it may be called *retardation*.
4. If adults tell their side of "the" story, it may be called an attempt at *clarification*, whereas when children attempt to tell their side of the story, it may be referred to as *talking back*.
5. If an adult raises his voice in anger, we call it *maintaining control*; however, if a child raises his or her voice, this may be referred to as a *temper tantrum*.
6. If adults behave in an unusual way, they may well be called *unique*, but children who so behave, may be admonished and considered for *psychological evaluation*.

POSITIVE REINFORCEMENT

It is clear that a positive approach to teaching and learning is of primary importance. Everyone has come to accept praise over punishment in the serious business of education. Teachers who give specific directions, look for good behavior, praise effectively, and use appropriate nonverbal reinforcers. As they model good behavior, they find that they make a dramatic difference in their classroom where positive reinforcement works for more effective classroom discipline (McDaniel, 1987). This is motivating.

But reinforcement is only a part of the larger field of motivation. Researchers (Bill, 1982; Bloom, 1982; Deci, 1975; Garbarino, 1981; Lepper & Greene, 1978; Maehr & Kleiber, 1981) have investigated many of the cogent dynamics of this related field of teaching and learning. Despite some degree of conflict among scholars, there is acknowledgment among current researchers that motivation is not unidimensional; simply stated, motivation can be internal or external, intrinsic or extrinsic. Defined as a constant thing, it is said that motivation does not change except slowly and over a long period of time. Some persons suggest that it is a personality trait, remaining relatively stable throughout life. The field awaits further study, especially in relation to the declining birthrates and the aging of a baby-boom population, which is causing the graying of the United States and its impact on the behavior of the young. Whether or not so, many teachers think of self-motivation as the best; that needs, desires, interests, and efforts come from within a person and can trigger far more learning than other influences.

For the purpose of this book, concerns here are with the importance of perceptions which students have about their own ability to succeed at a task if they try, and under what conditions would students have the best opportunity to learn or change, or behave as intelligently as possible and to exercise the most amount of self-control that is in tune with values. Moreover, another concern here is with the fact that students are different and, considering there is no best way of teaching, nor one best set of curriculum materials for all students, there is the awesome responsibility that teachers must learn to respond in different ways to different students.

Teachers can help students learn to want to learn, in much the same way that they can help students learn to read. At first, teachers have to accept students motivational levels, whatever they are; and they must adapt instructional methods, techniques, strategies, and materials to those levels, whatever they are. Teachers must vary those factors (time, subject-matter, topics, sequence of information, kinds of structure employed) over which they have control (Lepper & Greene, 1978). More specifically, there are promising teacher approaches or methods that may be used to motivate students, generally in classrooms (Davis, 1977), taking into consideration such factors as internal motivation, external motivation, personality or environment, the classroom climate, teacher-student expectation, student acceptance, rewards, and punishment. Thus:

1. Teachers should show interest and concern in student work, and give personal help when needed.
2. Teachers should be clear and make materials meaningful to students' lives and future goals.
3. Teachers should utilize a variety of methods, principles, strategies, procedures, and materials, choosing each one carefully and working at a reasonable pace for students.
4. Teachers should plan their lessons well, being properly prepared, and they should make goals and objectives clear to students and show interest and enthusiasm in their presentations.
5. Teachers should fully involve the students through the use of individual and group assignments, small- and large-group discussion, as well as discovery approaches and projects and at times planning.
6. Teachers should use external motivators by appealing to interest and to desire for praise and recognition, good grades and avoidance of failure, and link performance with concerns for the future.

In addition to these specific teaching methods, there are the following strategies which border on the affective domain and have very telling effects. These strategies are specifically addressed to teachers and parents, who should work in collaboration for the benefit of children and youth (Reckinger, 1981). These strategies emphasize that

1. Both parents and teachers should encourage their children and students, clearly expressing their expectation of them to be able, competent, and responsible.
2. Parents should continue motivating their children in much the same way as they did when their children were learning to walk and talk. That is, parents should also request that teachers work with parents, themselves.
3. Parents and teachers should provide comfort and support when there are setbacks, anxiety, fear, and discouragement on the part of children.

4. Parents should accept failure, take risks, expect and allow for many trials along the way, but not keep track of them. Instead, they should celebrate the positive and appreciate the small steps to success.
5. They should record success and applaud it; pay attention, actively listen, especially to feelings; and provide opportunities for students to use developing skills.
6. They should set aside some time for quality attention and practice, not rush new skills; maintain limits, and distinguish between what is safe and what is harmful.
7. Parents in particular, the first and sometimes the best teachers, should enjoy their children, being more a guide, teacher, enabler, facilitator, and fellow learner than a boss or judge.
8. Parents should remember that their support, love, and example are valuable motivators to their children. Both teachers and parents, working as partners, must become oriented to the crucibles of the classroom, its problems and prospects, ever being willing to try harder, even risking failure in the process.

SELF-ESTEEM AND BUILDERS

Students generally know what makes them feel successful or good about themselves. A parent, teacher, caregiver, significant community other, or any member of the various publics of the ecological environment can get a sense of students' situation by listening to sentiments often expressed by them. Particularly in the classroom, students ask that teachers:

- Smile when you see me.
- Call me by my name and, please use the one that I accept.
- Listen to me when I talk; it is not enough for you to hear what I say. I need your attention in this interaction.
- Let me know that you missed me when I was absent from school.
- Recognize my own special talents, even if they do not show up on my report card.

- Give me a chance to succeed in at least one small way each day.
- Acknowledge when I do something right. Praise me, if I deserve it.
- If you do not like something that I do, help me to understand that you still like me as a person.
- Show me that I have options for the future, and that I can set my own goals with your support and cooperation.
- Encourage me to aim high and help me with the process. Thank you very much for the kind consideration.

In summary, it has already been noted that an individual draws much of his or her sustenance from the family or caregiver unit (Branden, 1969). It follows, therefore, that since humans are social by nature, individual emotional satisfaction is usually sought within the group construct. Thus, an individual may find his or her essence in the configuration of the family, because also sought in this context are such qualities as autonomy, cooperation, contentment, challenge, creativity, peace, recognition, security, and freedom (McFarland, 1988; Young, 1972). In other words, since emotional satisfaction is sought in the family, the viability of the family must be seen as having paramount importance; not only for its unifying influence, but also as a sustaining institution which provides, among other things, involvement, adequacy, and love. The breakup of a family or the creation of impediments that threaten a family's survival can have ripple effects that transcend the home and the community, and thus, touch the school (Billingsley, 1968; Cochran & Henderson, 1986; Coopersmith, 1967).

The shaping of interpersonal relations, which may interest or affect the health of a child's life, is often derived from complicated structures that are grounded in philosophical, psychological, and sociological theories. For example, it is understood that pervasive emotional distress affects persons living in economically impoverished areas (Arnez, 1973; Ingster, 1970). Relevant research literature consistently indicates that social stress, as an external configuration of events imposing severe adaptational demands upon persons, is not randomly distributed in society. Persons in the lower levels of the socioeconomic structure are exposed in disproportionate amounts. So are migrants who enter those societies with a different language and culture (Rogler & Farber, 1981).

Similarly, relevant literature indicates that the connection between stress and its outcome impact on self-concept, self-esteem, or the feelings that one belongs is meaningful and can contribute to individual development.

Conversely, and also of paramount importance, are those elements which enmesh the individual in socially supportive networks of family, circles of friends, socioreligious groups, extended families, ritualistic and, perhaps, therapeutic groups or communities which are better able to compete with and/or withstand the pressures of stress. A philosophical position is, therefore, that supportive networks mitigate the impact of stress.

Attempting to incorporate stressed persons into traditional educational settings requires persons with interpersonal sensitivity and competence. To bring such persons together into a big "educational family" requires first, a bringing together of the "other families." Thus, the school's community and the families it serves must begin with feelings of trust, understanding, respect, and tolerance that must be demonstrated and reciprocated. Many social problems often burden individuals, and while it is true that there are expectations that all parents should help their children, it is also necessary to be mindful that not all parents know how to help, even if they are willing to do so. Furthermore, notwithstanding the drives of maternal instincts, many often lack the necessary resources to do so. Readiness is very critical; school readiness is a reciprocal responsibility. The school should be ready for the child as much as the child should be ready for school.

STUDENTS AND SCHOOLS: READINESS FOR EACH OTHER

Unfortunately, many of the efforts to provide children with healthy and rewarding lives are declining even as the need for such efforts is growing (United Federation of Teachers, Bulletin, 1991). Children from poor families, whose members are growing and who, in addition to being poor, are members of racial or linguistic minorities, fall into the dual categories. This situation, a by-product of a variety of demographic, economic, and social trends, is reflected in major changes in the configuration of the family unit in the nation at large, as well as in the work habits of women. Both factors have combined to create new demands on public services for children and youth at a time when political leverage on their behalf is declining. Moreover, a great proportion of this group of the population is also known to have suffered discrimination and have, until now, been the least successful economically.

However, despite these many negative factors impinging on student performance today, there is overwhelming support for teaching and learning that would foster a holistic education, one that comes from collaboration among a supporting network of institutions (Bronfenbrenner, 1979; Cochran & Henderson, 1986; Sonnier, 1982). It has been observed in this book that the ecological environment of a child has a direct set of factors which contribute to the success or failure of the individual student. This complex of institutions—the home/family, school, and community—are all complementary (Adams, 1982; Dulney, 1987). But, more particularly, the high visibility of parents in and around schools has a positive impact on student attitudes.

Teaching and learning are communicative processes. Each participant in the transaction helps to actualize the undertaking both verbally and nonverbally. It is through the process of education that acculturation, or political socialization or the ritual of transferring the cultural heritage takes place. Implicit in this process are the cultivation and perpetuation of the values and norms of the culture. Learning is, in some ways, a process associated with inquiry and decision making, and wherever decisions are made, value judgments are involved, values are transmitted, and the child is being socialized (Cooley, 1964; Levy & Renaldo, 1975).

PARENTAL PARTICIPATION AND STUDENTS' PERFORMANCE

Parents' values toward teaching and learning, schools and schooling, and education in general, help shape and, thus, determine children's attitudes (Topping, 1986). Also, attitudes of parents are rooted in their own prior school experiences. Thus, when parents are active in their children's school experiences, either as "home teachers" or as supporters of their children's school efforts, the benefits continue to affect progress. Through their involvement, parents' behavior may change, especially if this involvement includes the children's learning experiences. Parents are known to become supportive and their attitudes seem to shape their children's school performance (Beane & Lipker, 1977; Topping, 1986).

Since parental involvement in practically any form appears to improve student achievement, training parents as tutors and teachers may make them even more effective, with the result that noticeable advances among students are discernible. But this parent-as-teacher/tutor approach is even more efficacious with children throughout, as the gains in the parental supportive role encourage learning. Hence, parental involvement in almost any form (as teacher, tutor, reinforcer, or supporter) can assist student achievement and, therefore, have telling effects on the positive self-concept of children. Training for parents is needed now more than ever.

SELF-ESTEEM AND ACHIEVEMENT

Self-esteem is the evaluation a person makes and maintains with regard to himself or herself (Briggs, 1970; Coopersmith & Martinez-Perez, 1977; Jersild, 1952). It is also the perception of the self which is reinforced by the self and others (Boles & Shavelson, 1982). From the standpoint of schooling, self-esteem is a critical factor in the issue of academic achievement. Differences appear to exist between categories of students who are characterized as high achievers, or gifted, and those who are classified as remedial, or at-risk. Defined as high achievers are those students who tend to be goal-oriented, task-persistent, and highly motivated toward achievement and success (Perrone, 1986). They are also considered interested in specific areas, multipotential, usually independent, self-motivated, early emergers, and extremely talented and highly perceptive (Kerr, 1986; Lovecky, 1986).

Conversely, remedial students are characterized as demonstrating poor performance, which results in deficiencies such as low ability, poor study habits, low motivation level, or deprived sociocultural background. Accordingly, they generally seem to have deficiencies in areas of mathematics, English, and reading. Such widening disparity among students generally raises serious concerns about public education, since remedial students tend to score lower on self-esteem inventories (Briggs, 1970).

The task of motivating students who are ordinarily not inclined to set achievable goals and, generally, to succeed at higher education, becomes a difficult one. In fact, it first requires that systematic programs be established in order to increase academic comfort and, hence, self-esteem, as a priority for success. Furthermore, in order that students may be helped to alter their perceptions of themselves, that is, improve their self-esteem, there must be specific acts of attention. There must be the provision of special counseling

Required: A Positive Self-Concept

and guidance; procedures must become an imperative in the curricular offerings of the school, precisely because self-esteem must be emplaced, developed, and enjoyed before progress can be expected.

How can the self-concept of African-American, Hispanic-American, and Asian-American children be improved at school? How might they overcome setbacks, and what may be done from a practical and meaningful standpoint to improve their self-esteem and, thus, prepare them for the serious undertaking of being educated? These questions are not to be misconstrued as putting the burden of adjustment on these groups. It is not about blaming the victims, for surely there are forces within the social structure that are as powerful, if not more, than the issues raised in this chapter. That all-consuming power is the institutionalized disease called racism. It is alive and well in the society, although most persons would prefer to think that it does not exist. But it does and wreaks of deleterious effects.

However, these affected groups owe it to themselves to strive harder. Logic points in the direction of utilizing the several publics at their disposal. This means incorporating suggestions about what home-family, community, and school can do, and of the obligation to take advantage of all available resources; to become citizens in a state of preparedness that allows them to eschew the ugly and pursue the good. Because, despite the incidence of difficult, negative circumstances, there is much that the support systems may do in developing and presenting motivational strategies, principles, and procedures. These are virtues which can be found within the structures of the family and neighborhood, the school and its committed personnel, and, above all, the special self which everyone carries with him or her to school every day. Meanwhile, the cooperative efforts of home, community, and school should

1. Help in providing pride and a sense of warmth among families along with motivation to support the children's education;
2. Reinforce for students and their parents that their collaboration is vital to the teaching-learning transaction, and that their rich family heritage is important for promoting educational and other elevating pursuits;
3. Provide information relative to the maximization of parental involvement as a vital aspect of community participation in the education of their children, their impediments, real or imagined, notwithstanding;
4. Emplace within the context of educational determinism some foundational issues for generating better racial understanding and appreciation of all groups within the educational environment, at the same time, giving due regard to more sensitive and efficient ways of addressing problems; and,
5. Develop a positive home/family-school-community environment which fosters academic achievement that arises out of regular attendance at school, full participation therein, and substantive support at home.

Altogether, in order to maintain interest and effect on the urban school child, in terms of fostering emotional development, positive self-concept, and hence, academic achievement, all players who are engaged in nurturance of children and youth must bring their combined skills together for the promulgation of the nation's greatest resource, its current children and youth, as well as the future citizens. Motivation becomes a procedure of profound importance which must become a vital part of any curricular arrangement that seeks to help students with their global as well as academic self-esteem.

REFERENCES

Adams, D. (April, 1982). New date on partnerships. *Pro Education*, 10, 12.

Ahlbrandt, R. S. (1984). *Neighborhoods, people and community*. New York: Plenum Press.

Arnez, N. L. (1973). *Partners in urban education: Teaching the inner-city child*. Morristown, New Jersey: Silver Burdett/General Learning Corp.

Battle, J. (1982). *Enhancing self-esteem and achievement*. Seattle, Washington: Special Child Publication.

Beane, J. A. & Lipker, R. P. (1977). Self-concept: Affect and institutional reality. *Transescence, 5*, 21–29.

Bill, R. E. (1982). *Education for intelligence or failure?* Washington, D. C.: Acropolis Books.

Billingsley, A. (1968). *Black families in white America*. Englewood Cliffs, New Jersey: Prentice-Hall.

Bloom, B. (1982). The master teachers. *Phi Delta Kappan, 63*(10).

Boles, R. & Shavelson, R. (1982). Self-concept: The interplay of theory and methods. *Journal of Educational Psychology, 74*, 3–17.

Branden, N. (1969). *The psychology of self-esteem*. Los Angeles: Nash Publishing.

Briggs, D. (1970). *Your child's self-esteem: The key to his life*. New York: Doubleday.

Briles, J. (1990). *The confidence factor: How self-esteem can change your life*. New York: Master Media.

Bronfenbrenner, U. (1979). *The ecology of human development*. Cambridge, Massachusetts: Harvard University Press.

Brophy, J. E. (October, 1979). Teacher behavior and student learning. *Educational Leadership, 37*(1), 33–38.

Brophy, J. E. & Good, T. L. (1974). *Teacher-student relationships: Causes and consequences*. New York: Holt, Rinehart and Winston.

Cochran, M. & Henderson, C. (1986). *Family matters: Evaluation of parental involvement programs.* Ithaca, New York: Cornell University Press.

Cooley, C. H. (1964). *Human nature and the social order.* New York: Shocken. (Originally published in 1902).

Coopersmith, R. L. & Martinez-Perez, L. (1977). Self-concept and attitudes as factors in the achievement of pre-service teachers. *Journal of Research in Sciences, 14,* 455–459.

Coopersmith, S. (1967). *The antecedents of self-esteem.* San Francisco: W. H. Freeman.

Davis, D. (1977). *Motivating secondary school students.* ERIC ED 137 263

Deci, E. L. (1975). *Intrinsic motivation.* New York: Plenum Press.

Dewey, J. (1902). *The child and the curriculum.* Chicago: University of Chicago Press.

———. (1916). *Democracy and education.* New York: Macmillan.

———. (1915). *The school and society.* Chicago: University of Chicago Press.

Dulney, K. H. (1987). A comprehensive approach for parents: Community involvement. *Illinois School Journal, 67,* 42–48.

Evans, K. M. (1962). *Sociometry and education.* London: Routledge & Kegan Paul.

Garbarino, J. (1981). *Successful schools and competent students.* Lexington, Massachusetts: Lexington Books.

Gibb, J. (1964). *T-group theory and laboratory method.* New York: Wiley.

Gibbons, M. & Phillips, G. (December, 1978). Helping students through the self-education crisis. *Phi Deltan Kappan, 60*(4), 296–300.

Ginot, H. G. (1972). *Teacher and child.* New York: Macmillan Co.

Glaser, R. (1977). *Adaptive education: Individual diversity and learning.* New York: Holt, Rinehart and Winston.

Glasser, W. (1985). *Control theory in the classroom.* New York: Harper and Row.

Gordon, T. (1975). *Teacher effectiveness training*. New York: Wyden.

Hallman, H. W. (1984). *Neighborhoods: Their place in urban life*. Beverly Hills, California: Sage Publications.

Hoge, R., Smith, E., & Hanson, S. (1990). School experiences predicting changes in self-esteem of sixth- and seventh-grade students. *Journal of Educational Psychology, 82*, 117–127.

Howe, L. W. & Howe, M. M. (1975). *Personalizing education*. New York: Hart.

Ingster, B. (1970). *A study of the concept of urban neighborhood education*. New Brunswick, New Jersey: Rutgers University Press.

Jersild, A. T. (1952). *In search of self*. New York: Teachers College Press.

———. (1955). *When teachers face themselves*. New York: Teachers College Press.

Kerr, B. A. (1986). Career counseling for the gifted: Assessments and interventions. *Journal of Counseling and Development, 64*, 602–603.

Lepper, M. R. & Greene, D. (1978). *The hidden costs of reward: New perspectives on the psychology of human motivation*. Hillsdale, New Jersey: Lawrence Erlbaum Associates.

Levy, E. & Renaldo, J. (1975). *America's people*. Glenview, Illinois: Scott Foresman and Co.

Lippett, R. & Schindler-Raiman, E. (1973). From goals to action. Paper presented at the California State University and College Organization Development Workshop, Long Beach, California.

Lovecky, D. V. (1986). Can you hear the flowers singing? Issues for gifted adults. *Journal of Counseling and Development, 64*, 572–575.

Maehr, M. L. & Kleiber, D. A. (1981). The graying of achievement motivation. *American Psychologist, 36*(7).

Maslow, A. H. (1954). *Motivation and personality*. New York: Harper and Brothers.

McDaniel, T. R. (May, 1987). Using positive reinforcement. *Clearing House. LX*, 389–392.

McFarland, R. (1988). *Coping through self-esteem*. New York: Rosen Publishing Group.

Mischel, W. (1973). Toward a cognitive social learning reconceptualization of personality. *Psychological Review, 80*(4), 252–283.

Perrone, P. (1986). Guidance needs of gifted children, adolescence and adults. *Journal of Counseling and Development, 64*, 564–568.

Reckinger, N. (1981). *Parents' record of education progress*. Canoga Park, California: Center for Educational Alternatives.

Rogler, L. A. & Farber, A. (1981). *Unitas: Hispanic and Black children in a healing community*. (Research Grant No. MH 30569–03, National Institute of Mental Health, Center for Minority Group Mental Health Programs). Fordham University Hispanic Research Center.

Rosenthal, R. & Jacobson, L. (1968). *Pygmalion in the classroom*. New York: Holt Rinehart & Winston, pp. 108–122.

Rothman, R. (October, 1991). Focus on self-esteem, achievement turns school into showcase. *Education Week*, 14.

Samuels, S. C. (1977). *Enhancing self-concept in early childhood theory and practice*. New York: Human Sciences Press.

Schmuck, R. A. & Schmuck, P. A. (1975). *Group processes in the classroom*. Ames, Iowa: William C. Brown.

Schutz, N. C. (1960). *FIRO: A three-dimensional theory of interpersonal behavior*. New York: Grove.

Scobie, R. (1983). Situational teaching: Fostering self-direction in the classroom. *Curriculum Inquiry, 13*(2), 131–150.

Sonnier, I. (1982). Holistic education: How I do it. *College Student Journal, 16*, 64–67.

Topping, K. J. (1986). *Parents as educators: Training parents to teach their children*. London: Croon Helm.

United Federation of Teachers (December 9, 1991). AFT pushes court suit for school funds: The union keeps fighting in court to make the city live up to its legal obligation to properly fund public education. *UFT Bulletin, 33*(8), 5A.

Weinstein, G. & Fantini, M. (Eds.). (1970). *Toward humanistic education: A curriculum of effect.* New York: Praeger.

Young, T. R. (1972). *New sources of self.* New York: Pergamon Press.

Chapter 8

SUCCESSFUL SCHOOLS: A PARENTS AND EDUCATORS' PARTNERSHIP

The school is an institution created by society with the main purpose of providing opportunities to acquire factual information, develop skills, and learn to think. The main objective of the school is the full development of each student's character and intellect, personal and social relationships, and academic achievement. Thus, the school is an institution interested in students as persons and their total development. Children, youth, and adults attend school to become successful learners; that is, to increase their knowledge of facts and skills and to develop thinking strategies. If learning is demonstrated in these areas it is said that there were desirable outcomes of schooling (Asche, 1989; Contreras, 1988; Nettles, 1991).

One important variable in learning is the school setting. The characteristics of the school have a direct impact on the success of its students. Learning and successful students are related to successful schools. Successful schools can be found in any neighborhood or school district. Some schools are more successful than others, although they may serve similar populations of students or be in the same neighborhood. There are effective schools in poor, middle income, or rich communities. A large group of students in successful schools comes from communities with limited resources, inadequate school facilities, struggling families, and deteriorating social conditions. The question arises, how come? The answer is that successful schools are dependent not only on the type of building, neighborhood, or students, but also on the commitment and actions shown by the principal, the teachers, counselors, social workers, students, and parents of the school, working together to reach a common goal (Asche, 1989; Contreras, 1988; National Committee for Citizens in Education, 1982).

An effective school is a place where principals, teachers, parents, and other school staff discuss and agree on the goals, the methods, and content of the curriculum of the school. It is a school where everyone involved knows what the short- and long-term goals of the school are; that is, what is expected of every child in every classroom in the first month, at the end of the academic year, and throughout schooling.

CLIMATE OF THE SCHOOL

A successful school has a safe and orderly climate. Parents and the community at large may ask how one can determine if a school is safe and orderly. A safe and orderly school is one in which students are working on their respective instructional tasks, such as reading and writing, involved in an academic discussion with the teacher or another student, working in small groups, working on a computer, or doing a physical, musical, or artistic task. A safe and orderly climate is also demonstrated when students follow rules already established, such as walking on the right side of the hall and speaking in low voices. During lunch time, students obey certain rules, for example, speaking at an appropriate volume and disposing of unwanted food in appropriate places. If the school has a yard or a gymnasium, specific rules are known and followed by the students as to how to behave in those places.

Successful schools focus on learning and provide an environment where all students can learn (Gottfresdon, 1984; Scott-Jones, 1989). This environment emphasizes for students the idea that their primary purpose in school is to learn. The school is organized in such a way that discourages disorder and disruption. Teachers and principals protect the classroom from interruption. Teachers are trained and are always prepared to avoid disorder in the classroom, the auditorium, the gym, or the school yard. Regardless of where students are they should always be able to meet as a group and plan activities and carry out these activities as planned.

Good behavior, learning achievement, and success go hand in hand. Successful schools develop policies and behavioral standards which promote a school environment that is conducive to effective learning and the encouragement of good student attendance. Effective discipline policies contribute to the academic atmosphere needed for learning. In general, students who achieve good grades are identified as demonstrating good behavior, fewer absences, and less tardiness (National Committee for Citizens in Education, 1982). A safe and orderly climate in school emphasizes:

1. *Regular attendance.* Students come to school every day unless they are sick or an emergency occurs at home. Parental support and cooperation is highly needed in this area.
2. *Promptness.* Students arrive at school early. In the elementary school, students need to be in school when teachers go to the yard, gymnasium, or any other assigned place to take them to the classroom.
3. *Respect for teachers.* Students listen to their teachers and follow their rules inside and outside of the classroom.
4. *Respect for academic work.* Students demonstrate that they take school seriously. Seriousness is demonstrated when all the homework assigned is done, when all the school tasks are accomplished, and when students come to school with appropriate learning tools, such as notebooks and pencils, and are appropriately dressed for school.
5. *Good behavior in and out of the classroom.* Good behavior means respecting the rules of the school. Students demonstrate that they follow the rules of the school inside and outside of the classroom. For example, students have to know how to behave in the auditorium when they are sharing that place with many other students, and they need

to behave in the lunchroom where they are surrounded by many other peers.

A successful school climate provides students with an adequate environment free of interruptions where they can work to the best of their ability. Every school needs to have a discipline program that includes the following: (1) a written document that reflects the values of the community, the parents, and the goals of the school; (2) identified conduct or behavior that is accepted or not accepted in the school; and (3) identified consequences for not following the rules and regulations of the school. Such document is prepared under the leadership of the principal and with the advisement of parents and teachers. The principal, teachers, and parents work together in preparing a readable and well-designed handbook to inform parents and students of the school's discipline policies. Discipline policies are consistently enforced. Students and parents are informed of these policies, and parents are contacted when their children violate the rules.

Effective schools develop and maintain high academic expectations for students (Andrews, 1987; Mortimore & Sammons, 1987). Each classroom establishes an academically demanding climate. Teachers promote academic achievement by providing opportunities for students to show responsibility and leadership and by holding students responsible for their own work, by communicating to students that they are expected to succeed, and that their ability to do so is under their control. Teachers do this by setting rigorous demands: (1) making clear, course content to be covered; (2) making clear, course requirements and specific instructional objectives; (3) regularly assigning homework with prompt follow-up and enrichment; (4) devoting a high percentage of class time to learning tasks with a strong academic focus; and (5) communicating with the parents of students who are experiencing academic problems, or on the contrary are doing excellent academic work.

Underlying this rigorous academic climate is a belief that all students can succeed. Thus, teachers interact with all students in a similar manner. They do not call on some students and leave out others. They prompt all students to correct or improve responses. Praise is given when it is deserved. Less able students do not receive empty praise. Parents, teachers, students, and administrators work together in making successful schools and successful students.

STUDENTS' ATTENDANCE

Regular attendance and promptness of students are major goals of successful schools. For academic excellence to be achieved, students must come to school every day and be prompt. Parents of successful students make sure that students attend school regularly. In other words, students are not absent unless they are sick or there is an emergency at home.

Successful schools are concerned about students' attendance. If a particular student is absent for more than one day, school officials should communicate with the home to find out the reason for the student's absences. Also, the school has a program to motivate students to come to school every day. This program includes emphasizing reasons why school attendance and promptness are important and the academic and disciplinary consequences of not following the school's rules with respect to attendance and promptness.

HEALTHY SCHOOL ENVIRONMENT

Successful schools are clean, healthy, and safe. The school needs to look like a place where students can happily spend six hours a day, five days a week. The school's physical appearance, ambience, and general atmosphere demonstrate that all the school staff cares about the school. Although the physical appearance of the school is very important, it is not the only requirement to have a clean and safe school. The authors of this book have seen schools that outwardly are physically deteriorated, but on the inside convey the sensation of cleanliness and safety. The school is clean when the halls are free of garbage, and the floors and windows have been cleaned. It is not the fact that the water fountain or a window is broken, but how long it takes to repair them. Each classroom in the school is sufficiently clean to invite students to learn.

Successful schools provide a system of safety on each floor of the building. For example, the individual assigned at the school entrance is trained to do an outstanding job in identifying and welcoming visitors to the school and is able to locate them while they are inside the building. This individual maintains an accurate record of who comes into the school, where the visitor goes, and when the visitor leaves the building. A safe school has systems for the students to follow when they are coming to school in the morning, changing classes, in the lunchroom, and leaving the school. Concern for the safety of the students is shared by every member of the school community: the principal, the teachers, the students, and the parents. Teachers walking through the building or the parking lot care about what is happening around the school because they are teachers, not only in a classroom but also in a school community. Teachers take responsibility for all students all of the time and everywhere in and about the school.

INSTRUCTIONAL LEADERSHIP

Instructional leadership implies that the principal is the instructional leader of the school and demonstrates the effectiveness of his or her leadership so that every student is capable of making significant progress in achievement as well as in social and emotional behavior (Andrews, 1987; Asche, 1989; Contreras, 1988). The first priority of the school is to make sure that all students enrolled in the school learn to the maximum of their potential. All individuals in positions of authority in the school need to make every possible effort for the students to achieve in every subject area. But the most important leader of the school is the principal who leads the other administrators of the school and the teachers to accomplish the school's short- and long-term objectives. Successful schools have successful principals who run their schools in such a way that promotes:

1. *The highest quality of learning and teaching.* Principals build the morale of their teachers. Principals help the teachers by creating a climate of achievement and by encouraging them to give the maximum to the school.
2. *A safe and orderly school.* The principal must make sure that the school is safe and clean and that all students follow rules and regulations, and that teachers are teaching.
3. *A well-planned and well-developed curriculum.* Curriculum is all the teaching and learning activities carried out in each of the classrooms and in the school as a whole. The principal, other administrators, and teachers share responsibility for the planning, development, and implementation of this curriculum. All the learning activities have a purpose and are carefully planned to meet the needs of all the students in the school.
4. *A strong parental involvement program.* This program includes a parents' advisory council which meets regularly and is advised by the principal about all issues of the school, including the curriculum priorities of the school beyond the teaching of basic skills. Does the curriculum include computer literacy? What is the purpose of teaching students about computers? Does the curriculum include sex education and/or drug education? The principal works very closely with the parents and the community at large to develop the best academic setting. This cooperative effort involves input from parents and their involvement in decisions affecting children.
5. *A plan to recognize academic excellence among students and teachers in the school.* The leader of the school emphasizes the public recognition of students and teachers who succeed. Every time that an individual does an outstanding job in a subject or in competition, or is chosen to represent the

school, that individual student or teacher is recognized in the school for his or her achievement. This recognition helps to promote a sense of school pride, emphasizing the use of school time for learning (Asche, 1989; National Committee for Citizens in Education, 1982).

Good principals have a written plan for their schools. This plan needs to include the objectives that (1) ensure all students will perform at least at grade level; (2) identify the specific content to be covered in each class and at each level; (3) assure that subjects such as science, social studies, art, and music are part of the daily teaching; and (4) identifies the reading, language arts, and basic skills of mathematics to be mastered by all the students enrolled in the school.

The principal needs to be knowledgeable about the methods emphasized in the school. Methods refer to the specific ways teachers present the material to the students. Small-group teaching, whole-class instruction, resource-room approach, tutoring, cooperative learning, and open classroom are examples of different approaches to teaching. If, for example, the thrust of the school methodology is to teach students emphasizing the whole-language approach, the principal needs to be knowledgeable about this method.

In summary, the principal needs (1) to be informed of everything that happens in the school, (2) to provide for the best learning environment, (3) to provide teachers with innovative and effective inservice training, and (4) to be an academic and moral example to the whole school community. The principal is the chief instructional leader of the school and, perhaps, of the whole community (Andrews, 1987; Asche, 1989; Contreras, 1988; Gottfresdon, 1984).

VALUING EDUCATION

All children are capable of learning and all children are entitled to quality educational experiences. A successful school has developed a reputation of valuing learning and academic excellence (Gottfresdon, 1984; Scott-Jones, 1989). This reputation has been gained by working together with all the school staff and encouraging parental participation. Parents show that they value education by: (1) talking to their children about school, (2) supervising their child's homework, (3) visiting the child's classroom and talking with the teacher about how the child is working in school, and (4) attending parent meetings to discuss issues related to the school. Students value education by: (1) attending school daily, (2) following all school rules, and (3) doing all the school work required by the teachers. Teachers and the principal value education by providing a school climate and school curriculum in which learning is promoted and manifested in all the different school activities.

Students attend school to learn to think critically, to be able to make generalizations, to evaluate, and to arrive at conclusions that are based on facts. They attend schools to learn and to become more knowledgeable about facts and concepts related to geography, history, and science. Students attend school to acquire skills, such as reading, writing, and arithmetic. A school emphasizes that all its students be good readers, good thinkers, and knowledgeable about the information taught to them (U.S. Department of Education, 1986).

To be effective, a school need not bring all students to identical levels of mastery, but it must bring a high percentage of students to an agreed-upon, acceptable minimum level of mastery. The school staff believes that the school controls the conditions that lead to success. The school staff and the principal are committed to the idea that all students can master basic skills. Therefore, every effort is made in school to expect the achievement of basic skills, critical thinking, and problem-solving skills, and to actively teach these skills using whatever strategies or materials prove most effective.

LEARNING AND ACADEMIC EXCELLENCE

Academic success is expected from all students enrolled in the school. A successful school is one whose students enter its doors mentally prepared to do school work. Students, teachers, parents, and the principal recognize that the main objective of the school is to emphasize learning in all subject areas. The efforts of principals, teachers, and parents are geared toward helping students to achieve and do well in school. The school has a plan to implement instructional practices that promote achievement. This plan requires that each classroom promote achievement by: (1) devoting time to clear and complete explanations of new material, (2) providing sufficient opportunities for teacher-directed, structured practice before students work on their own, (3) giving students corrective feedback if their responses are incorrect, (4) providing sufficient practice in new material, (5) closely supervising students' work, and (6) assessing and evaluating what is being taught to determine if students are learning and, if needed, to plan for more effective instruction.

Academic success is rewarded. Parents are invited to public ceremonies to honor student achievements. Recognition is disseminated through public address systems, bulletin boards, and the school newsletter. Individual letters are sent to students and parents recognizing students' academic achievement. A successful school is one that regularly sends parents and students messages (in the parents' dominant language) such as those in Figure 3.

The school's primary goal is the attainment of academic development, and the school's mission is to provide opportunities for the students to demonstrate their academic development (Cummins, 1989; Mortimore & Sammons, 1987). The whole school community celebrates students' individual and collective achievement. Parents are informed of students' successes as well as their difficulties. Therefore, parents receive praise when their children excel and receive help when their children need help to accomplish the academic tasks.

Figure 3
Examples of School's Messages to Parents

"I wish to offer our congratulations to you upon your son's election to the National Honor Society."

"Congratulations! If the word honor could be extended to describe an individual, it would be proper and fitting in your daughter's case."

"Congratulations! Your son's academic record, as well as his record of care and concern for the good of others, makes him an individual truly worthy of this distinction."

"Congratulations! I know you must be proud of your daughter as we are at the school."

PROVISION OF ADDITIONAL INSTRUCTIONAL SERVICES

There are students who, despite the school's best efforts, are academically behind in basic skills or socially lagging in their ability to learn in a large classroom setting. These students need special services, such as special education, English as a second language, remedial reading, mathematics, and language development. Most of these students learn better in small or individualized instructional settings. An effective school provides individualized instruction or small group services for all students who need special instructional and social development. These individualized programs provide children with self-awareness, self-esteem, and coping skills necessary to reduce the barriers to learning. These individualized or small-group instructional sessions provide one-to-one instruction and the students feel more relaxed; the teacher works with a student's strengths and uses and builds on those strengths. Also, discipline problems decrease, since teachers work more closely with these students to develop a positive relationship to mediate discipline conflicts and build self-esteem.

In evaluating school effectiveness, parents should look at how students in need of special services are served (Carrasquillo & Baecher, 1990; Cummins, 1984). Does the school provide a classroom for each group or is the teaching done in the school halls or in the lunchroom? Does the school provide certified teachers, or is remediation the responsibility of the paraprofessional? Does the principal supervise these classes? Do materials exist, and are they appropriate to the educational and linguistic levels of the students? All of these are important considerations in evaluating the additional services provided by the school.

RESPECT FOR STUDENTS' ETHNIC, CULTURAL, AND LINGUISTIC DIFFERENCES

There are students attending schools in the United States for whom English is not their native language, who come from different countries and manifest different cultural characteristics (Carrasquillo, 1991; Crawford, 1989; Cummins, 1989). For example, in 1991 the U.S. Bureau of the Census indicated that 20.8 million people (8.4 percent of the population of the United States) were of Hispanic background and most of them speakers of a language other than English. It is estimated that there are about eight million school-age, language minority children in the United States (Carrasquillo, 1991; U.S. Bureau of the Census, 1991). Children with non-English backgrounds live in every part of the United States, with heavier concentrations in the southwestern and in northeastern regions.

Although children in the public schools represent a large number of diverse language backgrounds, the single largest group is Hispanic (Carrasquillo, 1991). About 75 percent of limited-English-proficient students are of Hispanic origin. There are also significant groups of Asian (especially Chinese and Japanese) and refugee children (especially Vietnamese, Salvadoreans, and Nicaraguans). There are other ethnic groups with significant numbers, such as Haitians, Greeks, Portuguese, and Italians. These are students who, on school entry, lack the English skills necessary for immediate success in an all-English school system. Schools are meant to provide equal educational opportunity for all students, regardless of language spoken or ethnic background. All students deserve and need equal treatment. Successful schools make it their responsibility to promote equality among all students, since all students have the same right to an appropriate education in the public schools. It is unjust for society to provide language minority students with anything less than a full and equal educational opportunity in order to reach their maximum potential and attain rewarding and satisfying lives (Carrasquillo, 1991).

Successful schools respect racial, ethnic, cultural, and linguistic diversity by infusing this consideration of diversity into instruction and by reflecting it in the composition of the school's staff, in extracurricular activities of the school, and in the oral ambience of the school (Contreras, 1988; Cummins, 1989). All students need to have instructional experiences that include the study of the cultures and the contributions of different histories, including the struggles by which diverse groups have sought to become full participants in the American society (London, 1990).

Effective schools plan and provide adequate educational experiences for non-English or limited-English-proficient students. Adequate educational experiences mean that the school evaluates the students' linguistic strengths and weaknesses and provides programs in which the students' strengths are used as a medium of effective academic and social development (Carrasquillo, 1991; Cummins, 1989; Crawford, 1989). In some cases, it is required that the students' language be used for instruction or that a special program be implemented to teach them the English language.

These students need to be instructed in the language that they know best so that they can learn skills and concepts in reading, mathematics, social studies, and science in the same way that their English-speaking counterparts learn them. For limited-English-proficient students or non-English-speaking students, it is more efficient to learn these subjects by using their native, or dominant language as the medium of instruction. At the same time, they need a special program to learn the English language necessary for success in school. Presently, the two most recommended programs for limited-English-proficient students are bilingual education and English as a second language.

Bilingual education is the use of two languages as media of instruction for subjects in the school's curriculum. The primary goal of bilingual education is to teach students concepts, knowledge, and skills through the language the students know best and to reinforce this information through the second language (Carrasquillo 1991; Carrasquillo & Baecher, 1990; Cummins, 1989; Crawford, 1989). Bilingual education provides for the learning of English, since there are provisions for the daily teaching of English. Therefore, students are learning concepts and facts in their native language, and at the same time they are learning English. The concept of bilingual education is supported by the idea that schools may use the culture and language of the home to maximize learning for limited-English-proficient students (Bilingual Education Act, 1968; Crawford, 1989; Cummins, 1989).

When the school does not have enough students of the same language, but a significant number of non-English speakers, an English as-a-second-language program is recommended. These language programs use special methodologies to facilitate the learning of English through the curriculum. In other words, students learn social studies, mathematics, and other subjects using English as the medium of instruction. The teacher makes sure that the language and the vocabulary are simple enough to be understood by the students. The teacher makes use of many nonverbal and visual materials and techniques to facilitate the instruction.

Schools must provide a satisfactory education to all students, including those who do not initially speak the language of the school. By providing instructional experiences through bilingual education and English as a second language, the school is ensuring that adequate learning experiences are available to all students.

PARENTS' ROLE IN MAKING SUCCESSFUL SCHOOLS

Today, many schools do not reflect the described characteristics of effective schools. Today is a good opportunity to start an effective program of parental involvement in the school, to put pressure on the school leadership to improve some aspects of the school. How can parents help?

1. Sharing the information of this chapter with their children's school principal and with the executive board of the Parents Association. Parents can ask how they, as parents, can work with the school personnel to make the school better.
2. Parents can speak with other parents about the school's characteristics that need improvement. They should seek other parents' involvement and meet with the principal to get his or her approval and the teachers' cooperation.
3. Parent's monthly meetings should be used to talk about characteristics of successful schools. Information should be shared with the principal so that he/she can share and discuss it with the teachers and the students.
4. Parents need to volunteer to work with school personnel in areas that need improvement.

5. Parents should continue the dialogue with the principal and the teachers so that these characteristics become part of their short- and long-term goals.

In summary, effective schools are needed for successful students. It is the parents' and educators' responsibility to provide students with effective schools. As mentioned in this chapter, there are many components involved when planning and developing effective schools. Parents need to understand all these components and become advocates when educators are not offering their children the best educational environment in which to learn. Parents should become partners in the education of their children by helping the school staff in: (1) sending their children socially and emotionally prepared to learn, (2) reinforcing the academic efforts of the school, and (3) cooperating with school officials in making their children's school effective.

Educators need to be sincerely interested in their students' academic, social, and psychological development. Their efforts should go into making all students successful learners. To accomplish these goals, educators need to provide challenging programs to help at-risk students, limited-English-proficient students, academically average students, as well as talented students. Thus, an effective school needs dedicated parents, effective educators, and successful students.

REFERENCES

Andrews, R. (1987). On leadership and student achievement. *Educational Leadership.* Alexandria, Virginia: ASCD.

Asche, J. (1989). *Handbook for principals and teachers: A collaborative approach for the effective involvement of community and business volunteers at the school site.* Alexandria, Virginia: National Association of Partners in Education.

Bilingual Education Act. (1968). 20 U.S.C. §880(b) (1968) Washington, D.C.

Carrasquillo, A. L. (1991). *Hispanic children and youth in the United States: A resource guide*. New York: Garland.

Carrasquillo, A. & Baecher, R. (1990). *Teaching the bilingual special education student*. Norwood, New Jersey: Ablex Publishing Corp.

Contreras, A. R. (1988). Use of educational reform to create effective schools. *Education and Urban Society, 20* (4), 399–413.

Crawford, J. (1989). *Bilingual education: History, politics, theory, and practice*. Trenton, New Jersey: Crane Publishing Co.

Cummins, J. (1984). *Bilingulism and special education*. Clevedon, England: Multilingual Matters.

———. (1989). *Empowering minority students*. Sacramento: California Association for Bilingual Education.

Gottfresdon, G. D. (1984). *The effective school battery*. Adessa, Florida: Psychological Assessment Resources.

London, C. B. (1990). Educating young new immigrants: How can the United States cope? *International Journal of Adolescence and Youth, 2*(2), 81–100.

Mortimore, P. & Sammons, P. (1987). New evidence on effective elementary schools. *Educational Leadership*. Alexandria, Virginia: ASCD.

National Committee for Citizens in Education, (1982). *Your school: How well is it working?* Columbia, Maryland: NCCE.

Nettles, S. M. (1991). Community involvement and disadvantaged students: A review. *Review of Educational Research, 61*(3), 379–406.

Scott-Jones, D. (1989). Family influences on cognitive development and school achievement. *Review of Educational Research, 11*, 259–304.

United States Bureau of the Census. (1991). *The Hispanic population in United States: March, 1990*. (Current Population Report, Series P-20, No. 449.) Washington, D.C.: Government Printing Office.

United States Department of Education. (1986). *What works: Research about teaching and learning*. Washington, D.C.: Government Printing Office.

Chapter 9

SUCCESSFUL STUDENTS: ABILITY, EFFORT, AND PARENTAL INVOLVEMENT

√ Students' success in school depends on several factors: the characteristics of the school, the mental ability of the students, the efforts of the students in performing the school's tasks, and the parents' involvement in the education of their children. All of these factors contribute to students' cognitive development, academic achievement, and educational attainment (Cummins, 1989; Edmonds, 1979; Henderson, 1987). This chapter's main argument is that parents as well as schools play a key role in the academic success of children. Schools that provide opportunities for students to learn concepts, practice skills, and experience some degree of academic success tend to have more successful students (Cummins, 1989). Parents who are aware of their role in cooperating with schools contribute to their children's success. For students to succeed in school, they need some degree of mental ability or maturity as well as an individual educational and parental effort.

SUCCESSFUL STUDENTS

Ability allows for an accumulation of skills and knowledge, while effort provides for the amount and quality of the tasks students perform. Successful students do not necessarily have to be "smart." There is a misconception that lower ability students have to work hard to keep up, while students with higher ability need not to work so hard. All students can be successful if they work toward success. More able students and less able students should be challenged according to their abilities and potential for mastering the particular content being taught and the development of positive educational values and attitudes. Students need to see the school as the place to experience success. A sense of individual success is an important factor for enhancing students academic and social growth (Bloom, 1985; U.S. Department of Education, 1990). But what is a successful student? Successful students share the following characteristics:

- Value education
- Have a positive self-image
- Are aware of their own thinking process
- Are good readers and writers
- Practice to automatize learning
- Are motivated to learn
- Are culturally literate
- Are good language learners
- Exhibit self-discipline and organization
- Interact with teachers well

The following sections describe the above characteristics.

Valuing Education

There are indicators of the values of students that are most likely to influence their responsibility with regard to their school achievement and behavior. The ideals that students and their parents hold are more important than the students' socioeconomic and ethnic backgrounds in predicting academic success. Successful students tend to have long-term goals that stress the importance of working hard in school. Many studies suggest that students who rate themselves as hard working and ambitious and as having considerable control over their environment do better in school than others who score lower on these values (Cummins, 1989; Edmonds, 1979; Henderson, 1987). Successful students place a high value on education, are motivated to learn, and have a positive self-image. Coleman, et al. (1966), reporting on factors related to school achievement, discovered that a set of attitudes, including students' self-concept with regard to learning, success in school, and feeling of control over their environment, showed a stronger relation to achievement than did family background and social variables. Students who have high expectations for their educational attainment are more likely to apply themselves at school and experience success in school. Thus, students' educational aspirations influence educational achievement positively.

The ideals that children hold have important implications for their academic and social success. Success contributes to positive student self-esteem, which in turn translates into positive student behavior. Children who believe in the value of hard work and responsibility and who attach importance to education are likely to have higher academic achievement and exhibit fewer disciplinary problems than those who do not have these ideals. They are less likely to drop out of school (Aspira Association, 1990; Cummins 1989). Successful students are more likely to use their out-of-school time in ways that reinforce learning. They communicate to parents and teachers the need to attend school, perform all the tasks required by the teachers, and do extra work in order to receive high grades in school. These students are not absent from school except in extremely necessary cases. They pay attention to what the teacher says and reads, and they make sure they understand the assigned tasks or homework given. These students go to school to learn and demonstrate their interest by constantly challenging the teacher and their parents to provide them with learning experiences. If a trip to the zoo is organized, they ask the purpose of the trip, they take notes while on the trip, and they collect information on the subject.

Successful students are motivated to learn (Bloom, 1985; Henderson, 1987). These students perceive the work done at school not as busy work, but as knowledge and skills that will help them outside the classroom. They are challenged by advanced or difficult courses. The more rigorous the course is, the more students achieve within the limits of their capacities. These students set special objectives and interact with teachers, peers, librarians, and other adults in order to accomplish their goals.

Awareness of Own Thinking Process

Successful students are aware of their own thinking processes; they understand how they can better learn and use this ability to control their own learning (Hyde & Bizar, 1989). For example, when these students are reading, they understand how to read to increase comprehension and learn from their reading. When they study, they know how to study so that greater understanding and, hence, greater learning can be achieved. Successful students are good at:

1. *Understanding what the teacher wants them to do in a specific task.* When they are asked to perform a task such as reading a story, they mentally say to themselves: "I am reading this book to answer 10 questions given to me by the teacher. I know what to do if I cannot find the answers in the story."
2. *Understanding if the task is important.* There are different levels of importance in the instructional activities assigned to students. Students need to prioritize these tasks in order of importance. More important tasks demand students' immediate attention, since these learning tasks may be a prerequisite to other more advanced instructional activities. Unfortunately, in many instances, school work is merely busy work with no purpose involved beyond keeping students occupied for a certain amount of time, and students

feel the need to direct their own learning to more interesting and meaningful activities.
3. *Understanding how to study to do well in a particular test or task.* One big problem of the majority of school children is that they have not developed critical study skills, with the result that on the day of a test they are overwhelmed by the amount of material they need to know. Many students do not know what to study and how to study. Good students learn the content to be studied by preparing summaries, outlines, or any other organizational formats that facilitate the priorization of content by levels of difficulty and importance. They also know how to approach this content for testing purposes. Students do not necessarily need to memorize content if they have learned it in the first place. Learning means that students understand the concepts presented, the ideas derived from them, and the generalizations or conclusions formed.
4. *Demonstrating understanding or comprehension of a particular concept or content.* School work requires students to develop strategies to comprehend material presented to them. Good students know what to do to overcome the problem when they do not understand or comprehend a particular learning task. Good students adjust the way they study according to several factors, including (1) the demand of the material, (2) the time available for studying, (3) what they already know about the topic, (4) the purpose and importance of the task, and (5) the standards they must meet to accomplish the task (Bloom, 1985; Hyde & Bizar, 1989). In other words, successful students are in control of what is happening to them in accomplishing or not accomplishing a particular learning task. Successful students make sure their study methods are working properly by frequently appraising their own progress.

Successful students learn from each school activity. For example, when they are writing, they learn through that process (Wells, 1986; Williams & Capizzi-Snipper, 1990). They use the writing activity to develop ideas and to express what they are thinking. Successful students do not get frustrated easily. They persevere with a task, because if they find that a strategy is difficult and that a particular strategy does not work, they can identify other strategies to accomplish the same task. Knowing how to learn may not come naturally to all students. Through direct instruction, children can be taken through the learning steps systematically, helping them see both the purpose and the result of each step. Successful students show organization and self-discipline. Students organize their lives into general and specific goals. They know what they want to be in school and out of school, and they work toward that goal. Students become aware that education makes the individual's life better and that education improves society as well. This organization and self-discipline help students to have a school purpose, a community purpose, and a moral/human purpose.

Cultural Literacy

Students do a better job at school if they have knowledge and understanding of past and present events, terms, concepts, and information. Readers and writers are linked to the cultural heritage of a given community. Such knowledge and understanding are called "cultural literacy" (Hirsch, 1987). In the United States, people make up diverse groups and traditions, together creating a rich cultural heritage. Cultural literacy enables students to understand this diverse and multicultural heritage of peoples, institutions, and values that make the United States unique.

How much students know about a particular topic determines how well they understand the meaning of what they read. For example, students may have a better understanding of the novel *Don Quixote* if they have knowledge of knights in search of adventure and about the ideals that were valued during the Middle Ages. Some of those values were honesty, honor, and freedom. With this knowledge, students can better understand the character of Don Quixote—an idealized, but honest man. Every society maintains formal and informal mechanisms to transmit an understanding of its history, literature, and political institutions from one generation to the next. A shared knowledge of these elements of our past helps foster social cohesion and a sense of national community and pride. This knowledge is essential in school if a student is to be able to cope with the wide and varied themes and topics of the school curriculum and society in general. Successful students are usually culturally literate—they have a wide and varied knowledge of many topics and many issues. Therefore, when they read they are able to get more meaning from a passage; when they write they are able to say more about the topic; when they talk their conversation is meaningful and rich. Successful students have strong background knowledge in topics such as geography, history, politics, and social sciences, among others. How do students get this strong background? Students get knowledge by reading about many themes and topics, by writing about these topics, and by listening to others lecture or talk about these themes. Students' reflections on these topics occur when they do individual or independent work and when, in conversations, they relate present situations to their knowledge of the past.

Successful Language Learners, Readers, and Writers

Students learn language by using it for a variety of purposes and in a variety of settings (Cummins, 1989; Wells, 1986; Williams & Capizzi-Snipper, 1990). They do not learn language as an abstract system, but rather as something they can use and understand in their interactions with the world around them. Students' language learning is guided by the principle of communicative usefulness. In other words, students use language because it helps them fulfill authentic needs. Children master language forms because they help to fulfill their intentions. Parents encourage the development of function over form by responding to the meaning and function of their children's language. Language is a system, and students simultaneously consider both their knowledge of these words and their knowledge of language to expand their oral language, reading, and writing. Students construct meaning based on their knowledge of sound-situation correspondence, sound-symbol rules, word-ordering rules, and the structure of a story, or they transact meaning by combining this knowledge with their experience of how language is used in different contexts.

Knowledge of language rules is largely intuitive. Students abstract rules from the language data around them and employ these rules when using language. Children induce the rules of language from the linguistic data around them. They learn what to say and how to say it because of their repeated exposure to language in natural, conversational settings (Wells, 1986).

Language learning is self-directed. Students learn oral language by selecting what they need and want to know from the language that surrounds them. They learn, question, hypothesize, and try out language to learn as well as to communicate. Certain conditions are particularly favorable for normal language development. These are: (1) young children must be in an environment in which speaking and listening occur; (2) students need to be in an environment where oral language is used, and they must actively participate in speaking and listening; (3) students need personal reasons to use language and to learn more about language; and (4) students need to receive feedback from others about their communicative competencies. Significant adults in their environments must ensure that their language works; that is, that it has its intended effects. Successful students learn language, oral and written, to fulfill personal communicative intentions (Wells, 1986). Students learn best when they are actively involved in their language learning, when they are immersed in language, and when they are exposed to frequent demonstrations of the uses of written language in a variety of contexts.

In general, successful students are good language learners. For successful students, language use and function are personally important, concretely based, and free from anxiety. Students use oral language in situations in which they are comfortable. They are most likely to speak and/or listen when they deem the situation personally important. Students' language, for the most part, focuses on people, objects, and events actually present in their physical or mental context. Students make a direct connection among language, environment, and situation, enabling them to infer how language represents the world. As with oral language, students are most likely to learn to read and write in environments in which reading and writing are personally important, concretely based, and free of anxiety.

Reading and writing skills develop as students experience language in its various expressions—speaking, listening, reading, and writing. Although children tend to mature as readers and writers later, they are already developing as speakers and listeners; each skill emerges in concert with the others, and each contributes to the development of the other. What students learn from reading a book or writing an essay becomes part of the child's linguistic data pool, which will contribute to the continued development of other language expressions such as speaking or writing. Children learn to read and write by reading and writing. In other words, children need to spend a great deal of time reading and writing in order to become effective readers and writers (Goodman, 1967; Smith, 1983; Wells, 1986).

Reading and writing need to be ever present in an environment in which students have frequent opportunities to use reading and writing; to see reading and writing used for a variety of purposes in a variety of settings. Reading and writing develop together. Students regularly read and re-read as they write; and much of what writers learn about the craft of writing comes from reading. In general, successful students like to read and they are good readers. Good readers are those students who have some awareness and control over the activities in which they are engaged during reading. They use knowledge of the way the passage is written (i.e., its structure) and the content of the passage to increase their comprehension. They establish a purpose for reading, select the best way to read the material, and make sure they understand what they are reading. These students are able to distinguish irrelevant information from relevant information. They are not distracted by extraneous information. Good readers:

1. *Establish a purpose for reading.* Students, when confronted with a reading passage, know the reason they are reading the material. Good students identify the main idea in new information, connect new material to what they already know, and draw inferences about its significance.
2. *Select appropriate reading strategies depending on the material.* Understanding a paragraph is like solving a problem; the mind needs to be organized to identify the purpose or demand of the paragraph in order to define specific ways to read it with comprehension. These readers use strategies such as: asking themselves a lot of questions about the passage; knowing when to read quickly or slowly, silently or aloud; and underlining key words, phrases, or sentences.
3. *Monitor their activities to determine whether comprehension is occurring.* Good readers evaluate their reading to know when they understand, when they do not understand, and when they only partially understand the passage. Effective readers are those who are able to monitor their own understanding and take measures to deal with any difficulties that they may encounter.
4. *Develop positive attitudes toward reading.* Students' attitudes toward reading can influence their reading achievement. Reading as well as writing focuses on students' ability to use written language to fulfill personal communicative intentions, and not on the isolated drill of reading and writing forms.

Successful students develop writing competence in many ways. Following are three strategies commonly mentioned in the literature:

1. *Students are continuously writing.* Frequent opportunity for writing is the single most common recommendation for improving the written composition of students.
2. *Students frequently write on self-selected topics about which they have considerable knowledge.* Students can write on topics about which they have much to share with an audience.
3. *Students' writing focuses on meaning—to express meaningful ideas.* Good writers put aside their concern for editing, for correct spelling, and neat handwriting. If the product is good, students should edit it later for clarity and conventional form.

Reading and writing are transitive processes in which students use active strategies for constructing meaning as they interact with print. Reading and writing are transitive processes because they are always used and understood in a context that contributes to their meaning; and interacting with print to arrive at understanding is what successful readers and writers do.

Automatization of Learning

Practice has always been considered an essential part of learning in school. This idea is reflected by the important role attributed to various forms of students practice during regular classroom instruction, in theories of school learning, as well as in recent conceptualizations of teaching functions. The main functions of practice are the consolidation of newly acquired knowledge and skills, and increased automatization in the use of skills. A certain level of automaticity is regarded as an important prerequisite for further learning because it provides the learner with new skills for applying the learned skills to new situations and tasks.

Developing academic talent takes effort and concentration. The literature indicates that the length of time in which students are actively engaged in learning contributes strongly to their achievement (Good & Brophy, 1987; Swedo, 1987). This effect is well seen in professionals such as dancers and musicians. They spend long hours practicing the same steps or singing the same songs in order to master them. Students need to practice a skill to make it automatic. It is recommended that students practice, to some extent, what they have learned, so that the task becomes part of the students' academic world. For example, students learn to write by writing, and the more writing students do, the better writers they become. Students who are highly motivated spend more time doing homework, not because they need to spend so much time, but because they are interested in what they are doing, they stay on the task for longer periods of time. In mathematics, for example, students have automaticity in the four processes of addition, subtraction, multiplication, and division when each process can be done accurately and quickly. In writing, automaticity is achieved when students can compose with a pencil in hand as easily as when they dictate to another person.

Qualitative, not quantitative, factors are crucial for the effectiveness of practice. First, adequate physical and external conditions must be provided for independent practice. Students need to practice in a comfortable place with few disruptions. Second, the practice materials must have been adequately prepared for independent practice and they are of benefit only if students have already attained a minimum level of competency. Third, practice is more successful when students are monitored or complimented and supported. Parents as well as teachers play a key role in stimulating and supporting independent meaningful practice. Through their guidance, students will learn to value independent practice and will continue practicing until they automatize learning.

STUDENTS' INTERACTION WITH TEACHERS

Humans have important social and emotional needs that must be fulfilled before work can be accomplished. Successful students interact with teachers and other adults in a human relations-oriented manner (Bloom 1985; Good & Brophy, 1987). In general, these students: (1) sit closer to the teacher; (2) receive more direct instruction from the teacher, since the teacher, through direct interaction, knows them very well; (3) are provided with more opportunities, through conversations, to learn new material; and (4) are asked to do more work; therefore, more learning tasks and opportunities to learn are given to them.

Students tend to cooperate, rather than compete, among themselves. Many times, these students work through contracts between themselves and their teachers. The student makes an agreement with the teacher about a particular amount or type of work. The contract usually includes a suitable reward at the completion of the work. The reward might be a grade, submission of the work to a particular place, or just being excused from other more basic tasks. But students are always consulting with their teachers, sharing new information and concerns. For successful students, teachers are more than teachers; they are conveyors of knowledge. They are facilitators of the teaching-learning transaction in the classroom.

PARENTS OF SUCCESSFUL STUDENTS

At home and in school, parents and teachers must continue the never-ending task of helping and motivating children to become successful students and successful individuals (Henderson, 1987; Nettles, 1991). Schools need the involvement and cooperation of the parents. Parental involvement, a term derived from the field of early childhood development, implies that parents need to get involved in all aspects of their children's educational process: helping students to be motivated, to value education, to maintain a positive self-image, to become culturally literate, to be good language learners, to be good readers and writers, and to interact with the educational community (Henderson, 1987; Nettles, 1991).

Parents should not have lower expectations for their children or tolerate less than the highest standards of performance. As this chapter indicates, all children can learn if adults provide an adequate learning environment and provide enough motivation for them. Parents need to constantly encourage and challenge their children by indicating to them: "Yes, you can do that academic task, and you will do it." Thus, parents are contributors and facilitators of their children's learning process and when they become resources to the learning act, expectations for higher achievement become a reality.

There is widespread recognition that there is a need to restructure the delivery system of education in United States in order to prepare students to function well in school and out of school. Clearly, parents, administrators, psychologists, counselors, social workers, and teachers have an important leadership role in facilitating the academic success of students.

Educators need to design effective ways of helping their students to take some responsibility for their own learning and at the same time provide the best learning environment and teaching tools to develop successful students. Wells (1986) sees all educators as well as students as meaning makers:

> We are the meaning makers—every one of us: children, parents and teachers. To try to make sense, to construct stories, and to share them with others in speech and in writing is an essential part of being human. For those of us who are more knowledgeable and more mature—parents and teachers—the responsibility is clear: to interact with those in our care in such a way as to foster and enrich their meaning making (p. 222).

REFERENCES

Aspira Association. (1990). *Latinos and the dropout crisis: The community solution.* Washington, D.C.: Aspira Association.

Bloom, B. S. (1985). *Developing talent in young people.* New York: Ballantine Books.

Coleman, J., Campbell, E. Q., Hobson, C. J., McPortland, J., Mood, A. M., Weinfeld, F. D. & York R. L. (1966). *Equality of educational opportunity.* Washington, D.C.: U. S. Department of Health, Education and Welfare, Office of Education.

Cummins, J. (1989). *Empowering minority children.* Sacramento: California Association for Bilingual Education.

Dulney, K. H. (1987). A comprehensive approach for parents: Community involvement. *Illinois School Journal, 67,* 42–48.

Edmonds, R. R. (1979). Effective schools for the urban poor. *Educational Leadership, 37,* 15–27.

Good, T. & Brophy, J. (1987). *Looking in classrooms.* New York: Harper and Row.

Goodman, K. (1967). Reading: A psychologic guessing game. *Journal of the Reading Specialist, 6,* 126–135.

Henderson, A. T. (1987). *The evidence continues to grow: Parent involvement improves student achievement.* Silver Spring, Maryland: National Committee on Citizens in Education.

Hirsch, E. (1987). *Cultural literacy.* Boston: Houghton Mifflin.

Hyde, A. & Bizar, M. (1989). *Thinking in context: Teaching cognitive processes across the elementary school curriculum.* White Plains, New York: Longman.

Nettles, S. M. (1991). Community involvement and disadvantaged students: A review. *Review of Educational Research, 61*(3), 379–406.

Smith, F. (1983). *Essays into literacy.* London: Heinemann.

Swedo, J. (1987). Effective teaching strategies for handicapped limited English proficient students. *Bilingual Special Education Newsletter, 6*(1), 3–5.

United States Department of Education. (1990). *College-sponsored tutoring and mentoring programs for disadvantaged elementary and secondary students*. Higher Education Survey Report No. 12. Washington, D.C.: Author.

Wells, G. (1986). *The meaning makers: Children learning language and using language to learn*. Portsmouth, New Hampshire: Heinemann.

Williams, J. D. & Capizzi-Snipper, G. (1990). *Literacy and bilingualism*. White Plains, New York: Longman.

Chapter 10

PARENTS: FIRST AND MOST IMPORTANT TEACHERS

In years ahead, it is believed that parental participation in school affairs will become increasingly more accepted, pervasive, and effective. More than any other educational movement, the participation of parents, the first and most important teachers of school children, will inevitably produce dramatic changes in the governance of schools and schooling. It is felt that parents will become equal partners with school professionals in deciding what schools ought to, can, should not and cannot do. Similarly, they will become equally responsible for the failure or success of U.S. public education. For it stands to reason: without outside participation and support, schools cannot really succeed. They need help from without, and parents, it is believed, can provide it if and when given a substantive chance to make the difference.

PARENTS: SUPPORTERS OF THE SCHOOL'S EFFORTS

Whether their function has been exercised fully or minimally, parents have traditionally supported school efforts. They have held certain academic expectations for their children and have performed moral and emotional acts of support which served as reinforcers of certain basic skills. Thus, they have implicitly presented themselves as role models for their own and other children (Clark, 1988; Dulney,

1987; Henderson, 1986; Kagan, 1985; Kinder, 1982; Spring, 1991).

It was not until recently, however, that any reasonable, concerted effort was made to legitimize, by both recognizing and harnessing, the valuable input of parents in the functions of schools (Cochran & Henderson, 1986; Dulney, 1987; Gough, 1989; Pysykowski, 1989; Sigel & Laosa 1983). Now, many appear to recognize the cogent role that families and caregivers play in supporting the school (Chavkin, 1989; Rich, 1985), as well as in instilling moral virtues and values in their children and in instructing and reviewing their children in basic skills (Krasnow & Heleen, 1988; Rioux, 1980); in helping at school with a wide variety of functions (Coleman, 1987) and, altogether, in presenting themselves as a critical component of the school's existence, purpose, and function.

Part of this long, overdue recognition is reflected in recent research reports of investigated outcomes. One such work is that of Epstein (1988), who, in a guest editorial of *Educational Horizons*, delineated a model of five characteristics by which parents are perceived in their involvement with the education of their children: (1) basic obligation of parents to children and school; (2) basic obligation of school to children and family; (3) parent involvement at school; (4) parental involvement in learning activities at home; and (5) parental involvement in governance and advocacy. It is important to note that Epstein's delineations encompass a wide array of responsibilities, covering a plethora of relationships, including those formed in the home, school, and community. These responsibilities affect and are affected by decisions, service, governance, philosophy, values, and the like (Epstein, 1988).

These responsibilities are further broadened to include other aspects identified by researchers (Chavkin, 1989; Krasnow & Heleen, 1988; Pysykowski, 1989) such that in addition, traditional roles of parents as member-participants, now include the crucial elements of individual decision maker, using choice in the selection of schools for their children, as well as their participation as social network members in both self-help, school management, and improvement (Bell, 1976; Comer, 1980; Dulney, 1987; Henderson, 1986; Swap-McAllister, 1987).

But all of these factors notwithstanding, it finally comes down to parents who make the direct encounters with their children outside of the school. There is now much more support for the idea of some parental involvement in formalized in-school participation of their children's education. Such support has gained credence from recent research, which has found, among other things, that children basically perform better at school when parents are involved and that children whose parents help them at home and remain in close contact with their children's school score much higher than children of similar aptitude and family background, but whose parents are not involved (Henderson, 1987). It is also true that parental participation may derive its motivation from certain specific criteria if and when they exist within and among the communities of education. For instance, parental participation derives impetus when there is genuine demonstration that their presence is needed at school. A warm hand extended is a genuine, initial sign of welcome for a school unit.

Establishing and strengthening links between family, home and school is critical. Reaching out to parents in a genuine way is essential. In this respect, parents can serve several functions, such as keeping a liaison relationship with school and community as voluntary or paid workers, and performing as interested participants, not only as traditional cake sellers (Cochran, 1987; Henderson, 1986; Huefner, 1992; Wells, 1988).

Schools can create within their physical plants, parent centers with flexible hours that would allow reasonable parental participation at their own time and convenience. Through such centers, parents can be better able to negotiate a school's culture, help with other social services, serve as advocates for improved parent-school relationships, and support teachers and administrators. In addition, these in-house centers should offer parenting skills training as well as other programs that are identified by parents and school people as being needed by parents. In this same context, parents should be encouraged to act as catalysts in helping to develop relevant adult education programs which can then be offered on-site for parents (Epstein, 1988).

In-house education programs that incorporate the input of, for example, community support services such as those of the social worker, could help to provide much needed information about resources and their location, availability, cost, and the like. Parents can receive orientation as to how they may obtain health benefits and economic, medical, legal, and other community services. Although these concerns may appear tangential to the child as student in the ecosystem, in these in-house centers, the cardinal issue of child care can be dealt with through the provision of infant services, which could be so structured as to include items such as snacks and carfare, in a commitment to parental involvement in the sense that:

1. Schools must show a genuine desire to involve parents in the concept of parental involvement.
2. Effective planning for parental involvement must include honest dialogue which will allow parents to provide significant input, regarding how best to handle agendas, provide assistance, and needed staff.
3. Reciprocal or two-way outreach must be created between the school and the community of parents with the educational communities at large being a visible and viable partnership as well.
4. Simultaneously, the school must become both a focal point and a repository of many community services and activities, as well as the center of a massive, meaningful outreach base which funnels educational leadership and programmatic packages to off-site centers in nearby locations within the educational community (National Committee for Citizens in Education, 1982; 37–47).

At least, one of the many overriding issues among this plethora of concerns is the matter of parents being given more choices in their children's schooling; allowing for the exercise of greater discretion of parents in the tripartite sharing of responsibilities, along with the several educational communities. In essence, educational reform policies and administration are now leaning toward the acceptance of the idea that they are more likely to achieve their goals if they are supportive, accommodating, and fair to all legitimate stakeholders. At the same time, they are becoming more realistic in their understanding of the telling effects of school failure because the fallout is obviously all around for everyone to see (Todd, 1992).

Partnerships envisage and encourage community-wide participation which must assume part of the responsibility of school reform for those who would benefit most: parents, students, and teacher, as well as other cogent participants, including employers. Home-school community participants envisaged in response to public school reform must now, therefore, include parents as school volunteers, tutors, home-visitors, along with business partnerships, and parent-teacher home networks (Beal, 1985; Comer, 1980; Davies, 1987).

Educational excellence demands dialogue. It should set high expectations and hold individuals accountable. Excellence in education for the foreseeable future will require, among other factors, persistent attention, high tolerance for diversity and ambiguity, as well as a regular diet of creativity. These efforts will become part of the cost of underwriting a never-ending pursuit, that of making schools of pride and promise available to succeeding generations of all the people, not just a select few. If there is close cooperation and comprehensive expertise aimed at the holistic development of individual children through sincere and caring performance, it augurs well that there will be little limit to the transformation that can occur in education. At least, children may learn more, teachers may become more fulfilled, and parents will feel better about themselves and their children. It follows, therefore, that the school, home, and community must engage in positive interaction. Parents, in particular, need to know not only the dramatics of the media, for example, but the more mundane, day-to-day activities of the school's function (Heath, 1981; Spring, 1991; Todd, 1992).

More precisely, parents just simply need to be involved in school. And, teachers and administration must have the security and faith to believe that the more parents are involved, the more they will understand and, thus, support the school. Besides, collaborative efforts of education are reflective of participatory democracy. Parental participation influences performance, therefore, the time spent with parents and their children outside of the classroom, as well as teacher involvement in school-community organizations and activities, will probably result in better teaching and learning.

Parents' involvement can take many different forms. Recent research (Krasnow & Heleen, 1988) has laid five distinct types of function that are perceived as being characteristic of current parental zeal and overture: decision making, parents as educators, advocacy, school support, and parental education and support. Specifically, *decision making* means that parents and educators share in the process of decision making. Specifics here include, for example, that parental involvement is included in the creation of an individual education plan (IEP) for special education children. Another form of decision making may be found in systems that provide parents with some choices in the school or program their child will attend. Similarly, a parent serving on a council which has responsibility for making important decisions about a project or school is also defined as decision making.

In the context of *parents as educators*, reference is made to those things that parents can do at home, at school or, in the community to contribute to a student's learning. Such activities may include home-tutoring programs, homework helper projects, and volunteer efforts whereby parents assist teachers in the classrooms as well as in preparing instructional materials. *Advocacy* involves two kinds of procedures: individual case advocacy and class or group advocacy. Examples of individual case advocacy include a parent advocating or negotiating for an improved status for his or her child by meeting with a teacher and/or principal, as well as individual grievances of parents that are handled though administrative or legal channels. Class or group advocacy, on the other hand, occurs when community organizations or groups of children, such as those who are new immigrants or whose families do not speak English, try to change an operating school policy.

The concept of *school support* is seen in examples such as the Parent Teachers Association (PTA) and other cogent organizations. Such groups typically work to support schools in their efforts to raise money for school activities, provide information and parent education, advocate increased funding, and build awareness of issues that affect children and youth. Another example of such support may include school volunteers who help with such things as student discipline, attendance, or chaperoning parties. Finally, parent education and support programs include providing counseling, courses, or information to help deal with the stress of parenting adolescents; learning English; or finding out about available health or social services, or about forming support groups. In many ways, these kinds of parental participation coexist and overlap within institutions (Krasnow & Heleen, 1988).

Parental participation in schooling, whatever its form or purpose, is expressed as a function of the nature of the philosophical, social, political, and economic underpinnings of public education, training, and schooling. The fundamental question, what knowledge is of most worth, is one that every culture, nation, or state must philosophically confront as it grapples with its basic responsibility of preparing its policy for citizenship. In essence, the concern as to what schools ought to do implies that the various publics must decide in a constructive way what skills, knowledge, values, and principles graduates of schools should have and of the procedures that schools must follow in their delivery of systems of operation (Bastiani, 1989; Kagan, 1985; Spring, 1991).

Public schools emerged out of the dynamic of service to the community over a century ago (Kinder, 1982). Their delivery systems are still undergoing change from one that was modeled around a rural, agrarian society that no longer exists, to a postindustrial, high-technology, information-processing one. In the rural, agrarian model, school started at 8:30 A.M. (ostensibly, so that there was enough daylight for students to help with after-school chores). Also, summer vacation was given so that children, again, could help out in the fields. New realities now face educators, requiring adjustments in some policies, plans, and procedures. For example, there are issues within the context of philosophy, theory, and process of education that beg for change. There are such issues as working mothers and caregivers; a growing senior citizen population; a soaring divorce rate and the resultant single-parent family structure; the return of many students to empty homes or apartments every afternoon because school hours are at odds with many work hours, and both parents/caregivers are still at work (schools continue to operate on the assumption that parents are still at home as heretofore); that parents can easily and always get time off from their jobs to visit schools. Meanwhile, schools continue, failing to inform, for example, the noncustody parents of school activities or to send them report cards; textbooks continue to make piteously little or no reference to any life style other than the traditional nuclear family, the continued derogatory use of terms such as "broken homes," "at risk," "culturally deprived," and "disadvantaged."

The fact is that today's parents need child care, sometimes from early in the morning (about 7:00 A.M.) to early in the evening (about 6:00 P.M.). They need programs for their children on Saturdays and structured programs and activities during summer. They also need the shoring up of the quality of educational offerings so that the trivializing of the seriousness of education is replaced with rigor and challenges: the de-emphasis of "fun" in school and the incorporation of skills that are commensurate with the requirements of life in an advanced, technological culture. This kind of delivery system must, above all, be for everyone and of the same high quality so as to provide equity of preparation in the marketplace (Kinder, 1982).

Public schooling has become one of the central most controversial institutions. Parent select housing in terms of available schooling; politicians often voice their opinions on school issues; some parents judge schools regarding their patriotism or lack of it; some members of society argue that schools and an education will end poverty, while others contend that schooling as constituted, maintains poverty. But, undergirding all is the refusal to speak of the problem of racism with all of its social expressions and its implicit and explicit denial, while it continues its presence in every human endeavor in the polity (Chavkin, 1989; Comer, 1980; Davies, 1987; Spring, 1991).

A single truth is that, basically, public goals of schooling seem riveted in the three divisions or categories—political, social, and economic. In general, political goals refer to the attempts to use educational systems to mold future citizens, maintain political stability, and shape political systems; social goals attempt to reform society, to provide social stability, and give direction to social development; and, economic goals involve the use of public school systems to sort and select talent for the labor market, the development of human capital, and the plan of economic development. These goals overlap within the categories. For example, the goal of the elimination of poverty through schooling can be considered both an economic and a social goal (Spring, 1991).

Among the most popular arguments given for the support of public schooling are that education increases national wealth and advances technological development. The contribution of the school to economic growth can occur in two distinct ways. One is the socialization of the future worker into the modern organization of industry. In this sense, it is contended that the school, the first formal public organization encountered by the child, provides the preparation and training needed to deal with other complex social organizations. Within the context of this argument, the school is viewed as one of the important elements in the modernizing of underdeveloped countries from traditional agricultural societies. The second way in which the school is perceived to help economic growth is through the sorting and training of the labor force through the identification of individual abilities and interests, as well as the determination of the best type of individual training and future employment.

The goal of socialization for the workplace is found throughout the history of U.S. education. One of the arguments given in the 19th century in support of marching, neatness, and orderliness in schools was the preparation for coordination and regimentation required in the modern factory. Lining up for the class as well as marching in and out of the cloakroom and to the chalkboard were activities justified in terms of training for factory assembly lines. Today, however, the rhetoric coming out of the highest levels of leadership underscores analysis of the plan for the year 2000, suggesting that the purpose of education is the product of the exercise of political and economic power (Spring, 1991).

As taxpayers, we pay dearly for public schools and have every right to expect both accountability and improvement. Unfortunately, some persons, including school people, take the position that all that exists is bad and all that is proposed is good. But, there must be a balance; a marriage of some of the old with the new; the tested, tried, and successful with the new, daring, and innovative, if only because in the final analysis, the prime locus for improvement and the prime resource for change must be the individual teacher in the individual school. To date, this has not been the case. Teachers usually feel by-passed by the educational reform movement and believe that reform is something done to them and their students, rather than for them (Anrig, 1992). Would not the involvement of parents have an ameliorating effect on both perception and reality? The research seems to point in that very direction (Comer, 1980; Davies, 1987; Swap-McAllister, 1987).

BUILDING RELATIONSHIPS

Krasnow & Heleen (1988) argue from the standpoint of their recent research that when parents and schools work together, there are many implicit and explicit benefits to be derived from the collaboration. They point specifically to the following:

1. *Children are helped*. Research has shown that parental involvement improves students' academic self-esteem and, therefore, their achievement (Henderson, 1987).
2. *Parents are helped*. By working together with school people, parents improve their sense of self-worth and also acquire useful skills (Epstein, 1988).
3. *Schools are helped*. Some schools may become better places for everyone when parents and teachers understand one another and are working toward a common goal (Rioux, 1980).
4. *Communities, as a whole, are helped*. This means that participation is important in a democratic society. Where this exists in an unhindered way, communities turn out to be better places to live when schools are healthy institutions, educating all children, fairly and equitably (Johnston & Slotnik, 1985; Krasnow & Heleen, 1988, pp. 1–16).

Nonbiased, nondiscriminatory, and imaginative efforts are needed to ensure that these benefits are available to all children and parents, including students whose schools are found to be the very hardest to reach by ordinary means.

The process of building relationships between parents and teachers requires a whole set of particular dynamics. Although parents are generally supporters of the school's efforts, the very act of parenting itself may be a very difficult and stressful undertaking. In fact, both parents and teachers have demanding jobs that require them to have special understanding of and give assistance to each other. Meaningful parental involvement projects can bring parents and teachers together. By coming together, this collaborative effort may enable them to develop more positive attitudes toward each other. When parental involvement projects help parents by providing them with parenting and other skills, they are enhancing their ability to act as professional educators, too. Some successful projects show that parents learn about schools and how they work. They learn about what teachers try to teach in different grades. Some parents, for example, from different cultures discover how children in the United States learn in different ways. They are able to see similarities in learning strategies that educate through such procedures as trips, play, and industry.

As schools reach out and create opportunities for parents and teachers, new attitudes develop. Some parents who have had little or no positive contact with their children's school before come to feel better about schools and teachers in general. They also have the opportunity to change their views about the importance of their role as at-home teachers of their own children. In their involvement at school, they learn much useful information which enables them to help teach their children at home as a part of daily family activities. They also learn to see the school as a place for their own education. As a result, some take advantage of available opportunities and services by taking courses, training for a job, or preparing for a career, beginning with the General Certificate of Education (Berger, 1981; Swap-McAllister, 1987).

But paramount to all of these undertakings is the increasing self-confidence that parents acquire as they learn things of value to themselves as adults and citizens. Thus, parents often express surprise and pleasure at being invited into the schools and being treated with respect. This is key and a burning requirement in parents' repertoire of expectations from the school. It usually begins the arduous experience of trust between the two publics: the home and the school. Informal settings, discussions, and working together on projects help parents to see teachers as individuals who are concerned about their child's learning at school and also at home (Comer, 1980; Rich, 1985).

When these encounters happen in a spirit of mutual respect and give-and-take, reciprocity should prevail. In such context, teachers may be pleased to see how interested parents are in their children's education and come to understand how fallacious their perception may have been that those who do not visit the school do not care about their children. Teachers can then speak with feeling about how they have learned about the strengths and vitality of groups, levels, cultures, and circumstances other than their own (Huefner, 1992).

Teachers too, grow as they realize that they can teach other adults. They develop expertise along the way as specialists in parental involvement. They may even become coaches, as well as trainers, for their own colleagues. By working together, participatory democracy gets an opportunity to be actualized, as both parents and teachers struggle to translate the printed word of constructed discourse into reality. Together they can conceptualize, design, and translate their thoughts and ideas into meaningful, progressive action, all in the interest of children and youth, and in the context of shared decision making and governance.

But, most of these accomplishments hinge on parent-teacher relations (Davies, 1987; Huefner, 1992; Wells, 1988).

PARENT–TEACHER RELATIONSHIPS

Despite much of the rhetoric about choice, the fact remains that most children still willingly attend schools to which they are assigned by their districts. Neither parent nor child is consulted about the books to be studied; the curriculum comes from the state education department, garnered from a source seemingly distant from the persons for whom it is intended, and with scant objection to this process. Parents exercise blind faith that all will go well with the schooling of their children. While parents have opinions about what ought to happen in the course of schooling, relatively few do much to check up on the schools. However, parents tend not to know what is being taught in a given subject at a given time; similarly, most have only the vaguest idea of how the schools are doing in meeting the needs of children.

Parents can keep vigil in two main ways: by reinforcing the mission of the school at home and by monitoring their children's progress. But this effort, this reinforcement, must begin in infancy and be carried throughout, thereby demonstrating a sense of the value of education. Parents should equally work to ensure that their children grow rich in several directions. Families hardly count on schools to look after the educational needs of every child; they cannot take anything for granted about the future of their children, including the quality and outcome of schooling, especially given the nature of the society as one that is troubled by drugs, AIDS, violent crime, racism, environmental deterioration, and international competition. Parents must maintain vigilance; they must monitor, and cooperate with, schools for the good of their own children. This is, in a sense, a new dispensation.

In other words, it is up to parents to take charge of their own responsibility for the education of children. They must now help to build a foundation for their children's language development, to find the best health care, to make the most of the year leading up to school entry and beyond. They must strive to arm themselves with the knowledge they need to ascertain that their children are getting all they should. In addition, these efforts must be extended to include: meeting with teachers; observing classes; and reading the themes, tests, and homework assignments their children take home. As well, they must gather information about what their children are studying in each subject throughout the year. Thus equipped, parents will be better able to discuss schoolwork with their children in ways that reveal their children's academic progress (Beal, 1985; Berger, 1981).

A point of importance in this context is the establishment of a liaison relationship between parent and teacher. The classroom elementary teacher, for example, should become a parent's most valuable resource for assessing the progress of a child's academic progress. A wise parent should get to his or her child's teacher and establish a dialogue, lasting throughout the school year. A savvy parent, albeit a school-smart parent, should use intervention in a sophisticated or gingerly way, deriving collaboration without unnecessarily creating friction. Of course, this implies a reciprocity of genuine response from teachers, who should honestly demonstrate their interest in parental participation (Cochran, 1987; Walburg, 1984).

Much of the discourse taking place is made on the assumption that a two-way interactional process is at work. But given the nature of educational history, this may not necessarily be the case. Todd (1992) argues that for the most part, the parent-teacher relationship remains cordial but distant. Invariably, at a parent-teacher conference, for example, both parties may deal with specific issues, exchange pleasantries, and promptly end the meeting thereafter. Even though teachers generally complain that "parents could make our lives so much easier by supporting our objective," yet at conferences, this opportunity is seldom taken advantage of by discussing with parents any of the cogent topics (Todd, 1992).

In essence, although there is a degree of acceptance in principle that parents are vital to their children's education, and although parents are somewhat encouraged sometimes to get involved at school, the day when parents truly have a substantive say in the operation of the school is still in the distance. This is even more telling in the case of many urban schools where, sometimes, it is extremely difficult to get parents to participate in the Parent Teachers Organization (PTO). Moreover, even though some parents are capable of decision making at the administrative level of the school's personnel, they are not basically representative of the school's population and are already busy enough with PTO work. Invariably, they find rejection from some school people who question their ability. Parents must work with what is available, beginning with the parent-teacher conference.

THE PARENT-TEACHER CONFERENCE

Kinder (1982) defines the parent-teacher conference as a source of great anxiety for many parents and teachers as well, although it has enormous potential as a public relations tool. One crucial but often overlooked point is that conferences work best as two-way exchanges. A successful conference should be as informative for the parent as for the teacher. The teacher, for example, who approaches such conferences with this attitude not only puts parents at ease, but also gleans useful information for working more effectively with individual students. Preparation is the key ingredient to productive conferences. For example, before a conference, teachers should gather all pertinent records and papers, jot down specific points they wish to discuss, and have some suggestions ready that may help parents to be of better service to their children at home.

Parents should be urged by way of the school's newsletter and personal contact to prepare for the conference; it should involve making a list of issues that they would like to discuss. Parents may also wish to ask children for their input when preparing this list. Moreover, if this is at all possible, both parents (or caregivers) should attend the conference. In addition, conferences should be scheduled before or after work, in order to accommodate the growing number of families with both parents (or caregivers) in the work force and to encourage fathers to attend. As a further aid to parents, many schools now provide babysitting services during conference and seminar hours. But parents must also constitute themselves into larger bodies that may enable them to speak with a larger voice, rather than as individuals.

A major purpose of a parent-teacher conference is to exchange information about a child. A sharing of observations, experiences, and knowledge can help to clarify a child's progress or lack thereof in school. Meetings with a child's teacher are important. They allow a parent to meet and get to know the teacher, ask questions, talk about how a child is doing, and discuss how a parent can work together with a teacher in order to improve a child's progress at school. A conference may be initiated by either a parent or a teacher. Thus, a parent-teacher conference can take place:

1. *At the beginning of the school year.* A parent may make an appointment in order to meet with his or her child's teacher regarding the child's personality and/or cognitive or learning style.
2. *After the report card is issued.* Schools may schedule periodic progress reports, several times a year in order to be sure that the parents are informed, and to encourage discussion of the child's progress, strengths, and weaknesses.
3. *At any time, whenever a parent or teacher may think a meeting is needed.* Figure 4 provides specific guidance to parents.

Figure 4
Why Have a Conference

- Ask for a conference if your child seems unhappy or anxious at school or if you are worried or concerned about your child's academic, social, or emotional progress.
- Ask for a conference in order to inform the teacher if there is a problem or unusual circumstances at home, which it is felt, may affect your child's performance at school.
- Request a conference to discuss and clarify such issues as classroom management, discipline policy, teaching style, curriculum grading policy, or other issues which may affect your child directly or indirectly.

In scheduling the conference, if the time suggested by teacher is not convenient because of your job or family commitment, request a different time. Some teachers will meet parents during evening hours or early in the morning before school opens formally. Also, if you are not comfortable speaking English, request that the school arrange for an interpreter who is fluent in your language to be present at the conference.

Before Conferences

Conferences between parents and teachers are essentially exchanges of information. These encounters should be pleasant, and teachers should share important information with parents, exchanging ideas and establishing opportunities for questions and answers. Before a conference, however, there are specific things that both parents and teachers should do. The importance of preparation must be repeated often, and both parents and teachers should gather all pertinent records and papers, jot down specific points which they wish to discuss, and have ready some suggestions that may help each other with the children at home and at school.

Parents should be urged by way of a school's newspaper and personal contact to prepare for the conference. All efforts should be organized toward preparation for a healthy dialogue. Parents should, for example, first talk with their children in order to get some ideas for further exploration and clarification at the conference. These points should be listed and, in addition, parents should be so prepared to share with teachers information about: (1) the child's special interests and skills, as well as particular study habits, likes and dislikes, or inhibitions; (2) medical problems that may affect learning (e.g., impaired sight, hearing, or other physical, emotional, or psychomotor factors that affect cognitive style and accomplishments); (3) Recent experiences (e.g., death of a favorite pet or family member, or parental separation or divorce) that may affect children's behavior.

Such information should help teachers to understand, and therefore service, children much better. This is the essential responsibility of teaching individual citizens.

Moreover, if this is at all possible, both parents, or caregivers, should attend the conference. In addition, conferences should be scheduled before or after work, in order to accommodate the growing number of families with both parents (or caregivers) in the work force and to encourage fathers to attend. As a further aid to parents, many schools now provide babysitting services during conference and seminar hours.

At the Conferences

At the moment of encounter, parents should expect and demonstrate cordiality. A warm handshake, a welcome smile, and greetings that are truly meant are all quite in order. The warmth or climate of the meeting is critical here, and both parties have an obligation to help establish this. Once there and comfortably seated, parents may want to ask questions such as the following:

1. How is my child doing or getting along in your class?
2. Is may child having any difficulties? If so, what are they? How can I help? What may I do to assist while he or she is at home? Is tutoring or other extra help available?
3. What is your homework policy? What happens if my child does not hand in homework?
4. How often do you assign homework? And how much time should be spent on homework?
5. How often do you give tests? How is my child performing on these tests thus far? Is there some way in which I may help?
6. How can I get in touch with or make an appointment to have a conference with you again?

Whenever possible, both parents (or caregivers) should attend a conference. In this way, each party can supplement the other's understanding of the dynamics of the transaction. Besides, it is more efficacious when both hear the information at the same time. This process minimizes the possibility of misinterpretation in the recall. If possible, use this opportunity to compliment your child's teacher.

Considering that schooling involves three levels of pre-college institutions (i.e., elementary, junior high/intermediate, and high school), there should be questions specifically designed for parents with children at these individual levels. For instance, there are some questions for parents of elementary school chidren:

1. How well does my child work alone at school? What can we do at home in order to improve his or her study habits?
2. How does my child appear to feel about his or her own abilities and about school? What can we as parents (or caregivers) do to make sure that these feelings are positive? (Sharing impressions with the teacher at this point can be of inestimable value.)
3. Is my child placed in any special groups for, say, reading or mathematics? If so, why? In which group(s) is my child placed and who are the teacher(s)?

For parents of children at the level of junior high school or the intermediate school, the following questions may be asked:

1. Will this school help my child to choose a high school?
2. What is the deadline for high school applications? Can you recommend high schools and/or programs?
3. Are there any career awareness classes or programs available? (Here, parents may share ideas and information about the child's career interests. Such information may then be used as a point of departure on a discussion about career interests.)

For the high school student, parents may ask of the teacher the following questions for further clarification of their interests and understanding:

1. What kind of career counseling and preparation is my child getting at school? Does the school have a job placement program?
2. What kind of college counseling is my son or daughter getting at school?
3. Where can we get help in completing college applications? Where can we get information about financial aid?

School visitation is really a unique undertaking. Therefore, in considering the many circumstances affecting parents and their ability to attend school conferences, it is prudent that every visit be treated as an opportunity. At that time, quite apart from dealing with the specific purpose(s) of a visit, parents should take advantage of the moment to observe the notices and displays that are placed throughout the school. Special attention should be directed toward displays in the child's classroom, especially if the child's work is included in the displays. Also, parents should observe whether the school looks clean and well cared for. If it is not, the parents should speak with the principal and the parents' association about what needs to be done. In addition, here are some questions that may be asked:

1. What special room accommodations are at school? How often does my child use them? May I visit them? How do I get there? Is there a library, a computer lab, special art/music room? Any other special classrooms?
2. What is the absence policy of the school? What must I do if my son/daughter is absent?

3. What is the morning routine? Where do the children assemble? When do they officially enter the school building? What activities are there after school?
4. What is the discipline policy of the school? What happens when a child does something wrong?
5. Is there a Parents' Association or other similar group attached to the school? If so, how do I join? If not, how can I help to start one?

After the Conferences

At the end of a conference, parents should thank the teacher for taking the time to accommodate them in spite of tight and demanding school schedules. Courtesy should always be maintained throughout, including at the time of departure. The conference having ended, it is a good idea to discuss the issues emerging from the conference with the child. In other words, just as parents consulted children before going to the conference, it is similarly reasonable to have a postconference session of discussion. Parents should share what the teacher said and what was discussed at the meeting, while emphasizing the strengths and successes of the child. Together, parents and children should draw up a schedule or plan which they can use together to chart the child's progress. Such a plan may include (1) setting aside a certain time and place for homework; (2) checking the homework, but letting the child find the correct answers and mistakes; (3) limiting the child's television viewing and encouraging the child to do more reading; (4) establishing a reasonable bedtime schedule and monitoring that schedule; (5) reviewing regularly the child's specific school skills (e.g., multiplication, spelling, and grammar); and (6) discussing topics and/or events at home with the child.

The main point here is that parents should talk with their children about those issues which came out of the conference and which, in fact, relate to the child's own growth, development, and progress. With tact, the child may be led to understand that areas that need improvement will be worked on together, with the child and his or her teacher and parents. Parents should spend some time thinking about how they are going to put these plans into operation in order to help the child. The success of the conference depends in large measure on the action taken upon its conclusion. In addition, parents should keep in touch with the teacher—by telephone, with written notes, or by scheduling other conferences—in order to continue interaction for a progress report on the child.

If parents come away from the conference with a strong disagreement with the teacher, then they should call the principal and ask him or her to set up another appointment or meeting with the teacher to try and resolve the differences. Appeals are possible, although difficult. If the parents are still dissatisfied after the meeting with the principal, they may approach the superintendent; have an informal meeting with a school board member, or request time on the school board agenda. In some cases parents may even contact each official at the state education agency or petition a federal regulatory office. Of course, these are rather extreme measures, and one would hope that whatever the issue, it would receive an amicable resolution at the level of the classroom teacher, who is the person closest to the child and is quite significant in both jurisdiction and knowledge of the child's schooling.

Parents working together with the school is the best way to help children in school. Parent-teacher conferences can help one to discover school problems quite early, and thus give parents and teachers alike a chance to work out a plan for each child in order to approximate if not guarantee school success. When a teacher calls parents in for counseling about a child, it would be prudent that the teacher and parents discuss related concerns that reflect the school's general interests. So, quite apart from dealing with the special matter at hand, some time may be expended in the pursuit of such issues as: whether the child has a comfortable place to study at home; whether the child has a library card and parents take him or her there; whether parents exhibit model behavior by reading to the child; and whether the family or home subscribe to or provide magazines at home. In addition, the teacher should try to get a sense of the amount of time a child is allowed to watch television and whether the duration has a deleterious effect on homework; what interests or hobbies the child has; and, whether there is information that the school may extend to help improve the teaching-home.

Altogether, these generic concerns are part of the school's culture and its ecology of operation; certainly, they may be used by parents and teachers as points of departure in a dialogue that opens up opportunity for gaining insights into a student's progress or success. Parents may be helped in becoming more a part of the school's educational effort. The challenge remains for overtures to be made during those rare encounters in order to remove the surface relationship and, instead, to emplace more substantive interaction with parents going from the cordial but distant, to the more meaningful. Teachers who approach parents with these concerns not only put parents at ease, but also glean useful information for working more effectively with individual students.

PARENT TEACHERS ASSOCIATION

Parents must constitute themselves into large international bodies that speak with larger voices on their behalf. Since parents are busy people, getting them involved in organized school-related group activities takes special efforts. And because the rewards are substantial, the efforts are valuable. A parent-teacher organization that functions smoothly and effectively is an invaluable tool for any school, district, or system that is trying to improve its home-school communication network. One such communication tool is the Parent Teachers Association (PTA). It is an organization that has traditionally serviced parents and teachers in a liaison relationship. This school-communication linkage is crucial.

For this reason, the following are some suggestions that may help to invigorate a school or district's PTA organization:

1. Set goals of one improvement project per year, then follow through with other projects that require more human power than money.
2. Make special efforts to stir up some interest in PTA office elections. If there are some officers who seem to be somewhat entrenched for years, tactfully suggest that there be a limit in the number of terms one may stay in office. In other words, circulate the functions; share the burden by rotation.
3. Expand the scope of the organization's participation to include districtwide, schoolwide, and communitywide events, such as service, parades, or holiday projects.
4. Include leadership from the parents who should work collaboratively with teachers when planning such undertakings as assemblies and school awards. In essence, broaden the elements of participation.

In order to establish a strong linkage between the community of the school and that of the parents, employing good communication with parents may also include the following:

1. Invite groups of parents to early morning breakfasts at school and use the opportunity to chat casually, finding out in the process their concerns and asking for suggestions about improving the school.
2. Distribute fact sheets about local schools, establish comparisons, and share these materials with new residents of the community.
3. Encourage teachers to stay in touch with parents by phone and mail. Remember that parents appreciate personal invitations to school functions or inquiries about sick or disabled children.
4. Provide elementary teachers with special envelopes to acknowledge birthdays, anniversaries, illness, and death—events and tender moments in the lives of children and parents that should not be missed (Kinder, 1982; pp. 22–23).

A CO-OPING MODEL

For most of their involvement within and outside schools, parents remain essentially in the scope of giving voluntary service. Huefner (1992) observes that parent voluntarism is an idea that works. We know from research (Berger, 1981; Epstein, 1988; Henderson, 1986; Johnston & Slotnik, 1985; Kroth & Scholl, 1978; Wells, 1988) that children of parents who volunteer in classrooms achieve higher levels than those whose parents do not. This is also true for children of both affluent and low socio-economic backgrounds. However, in spite of such available information, current piecemeal and sporadic approaches to parents in school educational involvement does not provide a basis for continuing family involvement and commitment to public schools across the United States.

Whatever semblance of improvement exists over the tradition, it may be argued, comes from recent transitional adjustments. We are now in a period of seemingly rekindled enthusiasm and escalating rhetoric about the role which parents can play in public schooling. The involvement is part of a theme sounded by President Bush and the nation's governors at the recent education summit. This theme is also high on the agenda of business leaders and school-support groups. Parents are being trained in the workplace and at some child care centers. They are being asked to sign contracts, committing them to a share of responsibility for their children's schooling. And, in some communities, they are being given time off by employers in order to attend school conferences and asked to take part in school governance (Bastiani, 1989; Berger, 1981; Epstein, 1988; Henderson, 1986; Swap-McAllister, 1987; Wells, 1988).

Within the context of this change dynamic, Huefner (1992) cites one kind of model, "involvement that has been less widely discussed as a reform model, but that could hold more broad-ranging benefits if widely implemented" (p. 28).

This reform model is identified as parent co-oping. In it, parent co-oping is defined as requiring at least one of a child's parents or guardians to help in the classroom on a regular basis. Already in operation in some schools, many parents of young children have co-oped in preschool programs and thereby gained new insights into the developmental aspects of child rearing and positive methods of discipline. In fact, many parents are said to have co-opted in several programs across several levels and disciplines with much success.

In light of these successes, Huefner avers that with the cooperation of the business community, parent co-oping could be expanded far beyond its present use, although there must be the following caveats in place to serve as motivaters: (1) there must be general acceptance of the idea by teachers and educational administrators; (2) there must be general acceptance of the idea by parents and teachers; (3) schools must offer training for both parents and teachers; and, (4) the cooperation of the business community must be secured so that employees may have time off for school volunteering. In essence, there must be "a widespread societal expectation that parents belong in the schools, and a presumption that they will be there" (Huefner, 1992; p.28).

This refreshing view appears to hit at some very sound philosophical issues which until this time have been skirted. If, indeed, there is really a strong sense of commitment about the substantive involvement of parents in the business of schooling the state's future citizens, then it would seem quite reasonable to engage the support of other cogent institutions within the polity to harness the goals and bring them to fruition. Research in co-oping has shown this to be quite feasible. As part of the latter issue of parental involvement in educational participation—that is, attempting to bring the matter from the educational level to one of actualization—significant potential benefits have already been demonstrated and therefore begs replication and dissemination in an appreciable manner. In looking at the effectiveness of this model, one can note the following outcomes:

1. Increased parental understanding of the U.S. educational systems. For example, parents would derive firsthand experience with the strengths and weaknesses of the system and would thereby, be more likely to appreciate the contributions of good teachers and to accept some responsibility for the outcomes. They would also have a more informed basis for rewarding sound practice and challenging poor ones. Ultimately, the experience of millions of U.S. citizens in our schools could generate more support for public education.
2. Increased parental learning and better coordination between home and school. This is to say, widespread parental co-oping would create many more opportunities for parents to enhance their own literacy skills and to reduce what for some has been a sense of alienation from schools. It is reasoned that in its best operating form, co-oping would create opportunities for parents to be trained in effective pedagogical and instructional techniques and, specifically, how to help their children with homework. For many parents and students, it could enhance their disciplinary skills as well as their sense of belonging in the society.
3. Low teacher-pupil ratios in classroom and more adult supervision. This implies that volunteering would provide opportunities for more individual attention to students and more small group interaction led by adults. The sheer presence of more adults, hopefully more equally apportioned according to race, ethnicity, sex, and gender, could have the effect of solving some of the discipline problems in our schools and of providing to the many students who do not now have an abundance of role models, as well as immediate supervisory and guidance services, other than those of their current teachers.
4. And, finally an understanding by children that parents and schools are partners in education and that they share common goals and objectives for children and youths. In other words, just as elementary school children of school volunteers are often proud of their parents' involvement and feel an enhanced status as a result, so too can the potential support from secondary students be encouraged. However, because adolescents share typical feelings of embarrassment

among peers, it must be remembered that procedures must necessarily be modified for this latter group (Huefner, 1992; pp. 27–28).

As an extension of substantive parental involvement, parent activism will benefit the schools; at the same time, schools will find it absolutely necessary to respond to the pervasive parent-involvement movement. And, in order to establish good interface and satisfactory collaboration, school people will need new skills and inputs. Principals, for example, will need to shore up their skills; so will teachers and related personnel. All will need to understand the exercise of preferred concepts, implicit as well as explicit, in shared governance.

Of course, in the actualization of the process, some school people may become frightened and, therefore, defensive by the expression of parent power. Some parents may exercise their newly found influence irresponsibly. There will be need for caution during the period of critical transition, so that by the time the dust settles, a new, albeit substantive, coalition will have been forged and made stronger as more effective schools will have been established.

It is certainly to be anticipated that partnerships with parents will increase support; increase the schools with new, important and refreshing ideas; and make parents accountable for helping the schools execute their numerous as well as onerous jobs. While in the first instance, the situation may present itself as a matter of parents' rights, in the final analysis, parents' activism is really a matter of responsible action. Therefore, when this happens and it should, the schools, it may be said, will be in good hands of shared efforts at seeking solutions to problems and improve the quality of schooling and its ramifications.

REFERENCES

Anrig, G. R. (April, 1992). Can tests lead the way to excellence? *Education Week, XI*(28), 40.

Bastiani, J. (1989). *Working with parents.* Wiltshire, England: Dostesios Printers.

Beal, A. V. (January, 1985). Toward more effective parent involvement. *Clearing House, 58,* 213–215.

Bell, T. (1976). *Active parent concern.* Englewood Cliffs, New Jersey: Prentice-Hall.

Berger, E. H. (1981). *Parents as partners in education.* St. Louis, Missouri: The C. V. Mosby Co.

Chavkin, N. F. (1989). A multicultural perspective on parent involvement: Implications for policy and practice. *Education, 109,* 276–285.

Clark, A. (1988). Parents as providers of linguistic and social capital. *Educational Horizon, 66,* 93–95.

Cochran, M. (Fall, 1987). The parental empowerment process: Building on family strengths. *Equity and Choice, 4*(1), 9–22.

Cochran, M. & Henderson, C. (1986). *Family matters: Evaluation of parental involvement programs.* Ithaca, New York: Cornell University Press.

Coleman, J. (August–September, 1987). Families and schools. *Educational Leadership, 16,* 32–38.

Comer, J. (1980). *School power.* New York: Free Press.

Davies, D. (Fall, 1987). Looking for an ecological solution. *Equity and Choice, 4*(1), 3–7.

Dulney, K. H. (1987). A comprehensive approach for parents: Community involvement. *Illinois School Journal, 67,* 42–48.

Epstein, J. C. L. (Winter, 1988). How do we improve programs for parent involvement. *Educational Horizons, 66*(2), 58–59.

Gough, P. B. (1989). Looking to the future. *Phi Delta Kappan, 70*(9), 658.

Heath, S. B. (1981). *Ways with words: Language, life, and work in communities and classrooms.* New York: Cambridge.

Henderson, A. T. (1986). *Beyond the cake sale: An educators guide to working with parents.* Silver Spring, Maryland: National Citizens Committee in Education.

———. (1987). *The evidence continues to grow: Parent involvement improves student achievement.* Silver Spring, Maryland: Committee on Citizens in Education.

———. (October, 1988). Parents are a school's best friend. *Phi Delta Kappan,* 148–153.

Huefner, D. S. (March, 1992). Parent coping as a tool for reform. *Education Week, 11*(25), 28.

Johnston, M. & Slotnik, J. (February, 1985). Parent participation in the schools: Are the benefits worth the burdens? *Phi Delta Kappan, 66*(6), 430–433.

Kagan, S. L. (1985). *Parent involvement research: A field in search of itself.* Boston: Institute for Responsive Education.

Kinder, J. H. (1982). School public relations: Commenting to the community. *Kappa Delta Pi Forum,* 19–20.

Krasnow, J. H. & Heleen, O. (1988). *Parents make a difference: An evaluation of the New York City Schools, 1987–1988.* Parent Involvement Programs Report to the New York City Public School, Fordham University Graduate School of Education, and the Institute of Responsive Education.

Kroth, R. L. & Scholl, G. T. (1978). *Getting schools involved with parents.* Reston, Virginia: Council for Exceptional Children.

National Committee for Citizens in Education. (1982). *Your school: How well is it working?* Columbia, Maryland: NCCE.

Pysykowski, I. S. (1989). Parents as partners in educating the young. *Education, 109*(3), 286–294.

Rich, D. (1985). *The forgotten factor in school success: The family.* Washington, D.C.: Home and School Institute.

Rioux, W. (1980). *You can improve your child's school.* New York: Simon and Schuster.

Sigel, L. & Laosa, L. (1983). *Changing families*. New York: Plenum Press.

Spring, J. (1991). *American education: An introduction to social and political aspects*. White Plains, New York: Longman Publishing Group.

Swap-McAllister, S. (1987). *Embracing parent involvement in schools*. New York: Teachers College Press.

Todd, T. D. (March, 1992). What is the parent's role? *Educational Leadership, 49*(6), 88–89.

Walburg, H. J. (1984). Families as partners in educational productivity. *Phi Delta Kappan, 65*(6), 397–400.

Wells, A. S. (January 3, 1988). The parent's place: Right in the school. *New York Times Education and Life*, pp. 63–68.

Chapter 11

RECOMMENDATIONS FOR THE IMPROVEMENT OF PARENTAL SCHOOL INVOLVEMENT

For the past several decades, family life in the United States has undergone a tremendous transformation. In 1889, people were judged literate if they could sign their names. But that was the era of the farm-and-buggy economy. In the machine economy of 1939, being literate meant completing the sixth grade. Today, however, the postindustrialized culture of the information-processing age of computers and high technology requires a bare minimum of reading and writing skills at the high-school-graduate level. Changes in the workplace are so dramatic and unpredictable that people must be ready to adapt to jobs that did not even exist when they were in school. With 25 million citizens who cannot read or write, and an additional 45 million who are functionally illiterate (i.e., who do not have the reading and writing skills to find work), the number is said to be growing by more than two million a year. Yet in the postindustrial era, the majority of the people in the workforce must make a living with their hands and their minds.

In March 1990, there were 66 million families in the United States, of which 79 percent were maintained by married couples, 17 percent by females householders, and 4 percent by male householders with no spouse present (U.S. Bureau of the Census, 1991). One child in six lives today in a household headed by a female, and in this highly mobile society the extended family now offers less support. Many grandparents work; others live too far away to help nurture this youngest generation on whom the nation will depend only a few decades hence.

Education is the key to socio-cultural and economic life. Authorities cited in previous chapters indicate that the benefits of education show that youngsters who are educated are half as likely to have teenage pregnancies; half as likely to drop out or to be arrested; half as likely to be on welfare; and nearly twice as likely to go on to higher education. In such persons, there is the possibility of a good citizen. In the 1990s, in the wake of years of recession and re-analysis of international markets, educators, youth advocates, and policy makers are calling for schools to educate not only the talented students, the linguistically different, and the handicapped, but to provide quality of education for all students in the name of excellence. Increased community participation is needed to solve the problems of schooling and the education of children and youth. This chapter presents recommendations to national, federal, state, and local organizations and to parents in assuring educational opportunities for children and youth through more and better partnerships between schools, parents, and the community.

RECOMMENDATIONS TO NATIONAL PARENTS ORGANIZATIONS

Now, more than ever, there is a sense that upgrading educational policy, plans, and delivery systems has become a very critical concern. The pervasive defense among many scholars of avoiding the perception of academic failure is now giving way to more realistic approaches that include broader participation by all members of the U.S. schools and communities. The exigencies of the prevailing circumstances cry out for a kind of partnership whose time has come. Such partnership envisages and now encourages national participation which must assume part of the responsibility of school reform. National parents organizations play a key role in providing leadership and guidance to local parents groups and to educational agencies by recommending successful strategies to provide equal educational opportunities for all students.

Communities throughout the country are beginning to realize the amount of change that can be brought about through cooperative efforts. A major goal of communities focuses on quality education for students. Through the concept of community education, citizen participation is most fully developed. This concept has its roots in the belief that schools belong to the community and that learning also occurs outside the classroom. National organizations should work closely and cooperatively with local educational groups and leaders in providing training in developing school power and community resources. This national training will provide community action and participation in the shaping of school systems. National organizations can provide social support and advocacy roles. Since national parents organizations gather and develop information from a nationwide network of sources in education, government, and citizen/parent organizations, they can disseminate this information to local organizations throughout the country. This network role needs to be accessible to local organizations that ask for these services as well to those local organizations that because of ignorance do not request these services. National organizations should reach local organizations in need. They should not sit and wait for successful local organizations to request information or advice. They need to have a committee whose main function is to identify parental groups that lack leadership or organizational skills and volunteer to help them improve the management of local parent organizations.

RECOMMENDATIONS TO FEDERAL AND STATE AGENCIES

Education is a main responsibility of federal and state educational agencies, and federal and state legislators as well as their representatives in education departments control many of the requirements imposed on education. These individuals play a main role in advising and recommending to the federal or state agencies how to allocate resources, in addition to providing recommendations for the instruction and curriculum as well as how to access citizen and organizational participation in the educational process. Unfortunately, many legislators or their representatives do not have the necessary educational background; however, they decide and have the final word in many situations. Koppman (1989) said that educators and parents have indicated and accepted an educational pyramid that looks like the one in the left (A) rather than the pyramid to the right (B).

Pyramid A		*Pyramid B*
Legislators		Parents
Media		Students
School boards	rather than:	Teachers
Administrators		Administrators
Teachers		School boards
Students		Media
Parents		Legislators

Koppman suggested that "parents and students would be expected to take a major role in the education process, with the teachers and administrators providing academic training. School boards, media and legislators would provide the base, the foundation upon which education can be built" (p. 3). Federal and state educational agencies need to adapt the following four practices:

1. Agencies need to allocate resources equally to eliminate disadvantages of students' access to services (Nettles, 1991). Resources need to be allocated to all schools, including schools attended primarily by low-income youths. The authors of this book have visited many urban schools where students do not have textbooks or even classrooms. However, many suburban schools enjoyed textbooks, supplementary books, well-maintained classrooms, computers in each classroom, as well as many recreational resources. It is unfair not to provide equal educational opportunities for all students. However, when federal and state agencies evaluate students' academic performance, they recommend the same testing and evaluation measurement of scores for all students.
2. There is a need to provide incentives for effort and achievement, thereby encouraging students to invest in constructive pursuits. Students are always listening to the same story: "According to national testing norms, students are doing unsatisfactory work." We recommend that students receive some types of incentives for good school performance. What has happened lately is that because of state and federal agencies' financial difficulties, the little financial resources that once existed have been decreased. For example, New York State used to give a small college scholarship to students performing above average on the college admission test. This financial incentive has been reduced to a minimum. Incentives may include personalized letters to students and parents, certificates, and free coupons, in addition to scholarships or other financial assistance.
3. There is a significant number of students who need academic, psychological, or counseling assistance; students who need or want such assistance should be able to receive it. Many parents cannot provide such assistance due to lack of resources or because of ignorance. Federal and state agencies need to be more receptive to these needs and create regional offices whose main purpose is to help parents and students. For example, the New York City United Federation of Teachers has an after-school program to help students who need assistance with homework. The student in need calls and a teacher helps him or her with the

homework. These services are extremely needed, especially in low socio-economic neighborhoods.
4. Students and schools need social support. Teachers and administrators need assistance in providing students with the social support they need to perform well in school. Today, when a significant number of parents are drug addicts or alcoholics, or are suffering from AIDS or other social or physical illness, schools, more than ever, confront the problem of being more than facilitators of knowledge. The school cannot do the work alone. Part-time or itinerant social workers, nurses, and psychologists cannot do effective work alone. Federal and state educational agencies need to see these resources as of primary importance in the education of all children, and provide funds so that they be available in every school in the country.

RECOMMENDATIONS TO LOCAL COMMUNITY SCHOOL BOARDS

Communities have always played important roles in students' academic, intellectual, and psychological development. These communities must also play an active role in the implementation of educational programs. This involvement starts at the decision-making level and continues until the programs are implemented in the home, where individual parents show their children that they fully support their educational efforts. If the parents are ill-informed of the program's intent and practice, they will not trust it. If they do not trust it, they will exhibit disapproval to their children. If the children feel that their parents have no faith in their education, their learning will be severely hindered. The authors believe that to effect the kind of attitudinal change required to achieve this objective, the educational system must involve communities and parents in a meaningful manner. One very effective tool is the local community school board, which formalizes the relationship between parents and educators. Informed and effective community school boards will produce schools that are responsive to parent and community concerns. More specifically, an active and informed council bases its decisions on thoughtful planning rather than on the limited options provided by schools, and therefore is more effective in promoting a better learning environment for children. Parents serving on the community school board recommend program changes, provide community input for the program's administration, and plot future developments for the program and their children. Therefore, most members of the community school board should be parents.

Local community school board members are representatives of the public which elected them to office. Local school boards play a very important function in assisting students in their intellectual development, and in learning the rules and values that govern social relationships in the community. As representatives of citizens, they are responsible for ensuring community participation in the areas of school reform and improvements, legal action, as well as fiscal responsibility, and evaluation of the quality of instruction provided. Citizen and parental participation on school governing boards may produce changes in the curriculum or in teacher attitudes toward students. These changes, in turn, may affect student achievement levels. The following are recommendations the authors would like to present to local community school boards for improving the quality of education.

1. Local community school boards need to identify practices that promote change. There are general guides for community action and handbooks that suggest specific actions to link schools and students with other entities of the community (Asche, 1989). One important aspect is citizen participation in school decision making (Williams, 1988).
2. There is a tremendous need to develop partnerships between schools and community entities, such as businesses, social service agencies, universities, cultural institutions, and community-based organizations (Nettles, 1991). School boards should involve all these agencies in the discussions of

finding better ways and means to educate all children of the community. School boards need to provide parents with written materials prepared for board meetings, and should also provide the public with accurate and detailed information about the deliberations and decisions of the school board.
3. The home-school-community partnerships must include broad educational resources and programs, such as school volunteers, tutoring, home visits, business partnerships, parent-teacher-home visitations, and parental group conferences. Community school boards should be amenable to the idea of providing access to information or other resources when needed.
4. Connecting schools, parents, and community leaders for the exchange of research and productive information is an important step in improving community school boards. They can accommodate for trade-offs of time, space, and educational goods in order to better capitalize on the available special attributes and resources that would altogether empower individuals and groups to derive increased control over their own lives.

RECOMMENDATIONS TO PARENTS

It is often thought that parenting is a natural talent, a spontaneously acquired, unlearned skill. Others say that parenting is learned early, as language is, and largely through one's own parents' example. But everyone agrees that parenting is a very serious responsibility and the ways adults practice parenting affects the psychological, social, and educational growth of their children. Parental involvement contributes to quality in education. Quality education encompasses the opportunities given to students to acquire usable knowledge, develop problem-solving skills, inquiry skills, an appreciation of the arts, personal and social responsibility, self-respect, and respect for others (Contreras, 1988; Stallings, 1986). The family and parents are a cornerstone of the foundation of American education. The "curriculum" of the home is found to be twice as predictive of academic learning as family socio-economic status. Parenting is therefore important.

Children 18 years or younger spend approximately 13 percent of their waking hours in school and the balance of the waking hours under the control of their parents (Contreras, 1988). As parents work with national and state community organizations and with school agencies, they can develop an active base of citizen support and a menu of school- and community-based activities to improve in students' attendance, academic motivation, sense of responsibility, grades, and tests scores (Nettles, 1991). This is not an easy task. Roles of the various parents need to be defined and mechanisms for the sustained involvement of parents identified. It is a curriculum that promotes parent-child conversations about everyday events, encouragement, discussion of leisure reading to accomplish long-term goals, expression of affection, and direct interest in the child's education.

Parents need to be involved in instruction, in social interactions in the home, and in the wider community in providing children with opportunities to learn. It is important that the child's educational program be favorably accepted and reinforced at home. Parents need to reinforce the school's efforts of taking an active role in their children's education. Through pertinent tasks and strategies, parents can help their children develop the literacy skills and behaviors needed to perform in schools and in daily communication (Asche, 1989; Nettles, 1991; Williams, 1989). The role of parents in informal and structured instruction is of primordial importance. Parental participation in children's efforts to learn in schools as well as in the broader community can have positive efforts on students' school achievement.

RECOMMENDATIONS FOR THE INCLUSION OF PARENTS FROM DIVERSE CULTURAL AND LINGUISTIC BACKGROUNDS

Educational excellence demands challenges; it sets high expectations and holds individuals accountable. Excellence in education will require for its achievement, our persistent attention and high tolerance for diversity and ambiguity, as well as opportunities for creativity. It is only at such cost that we can underwrite a never-ending pursuit: making schools available to succeeding generations of all the people, not just a select few.

Including parents from diverse linguistic and cultural environments will help to: (1) build rapport with parents through adequate communication; (2) assist parents or other interested members of the community to understand the school curriculum; (3) solicit parental help in developing the instructional program; (4) gain parental support in implementing the program; (5) clarify conflicting values and goals; and (6) provide literacy training in the school, so that parents can tutor children in the native language.

Parents must be able to determine the kinds of language programs their children will receive (e.g., English as a second language or bilingual education), the duration of those programs, and the comprehensiveness of the programs as part of a total school effort to promote bilingualism and multiculturalism. This means that parents, in effect, must provide guidance to schools on the implementation of language policy at the local school level. However, in order to fill an important role as a local language policy group, parents must have full access to information about the total school program, not just the programs designed to serve the language needs of their children. They must be able to plan with school personnel for the integration of the educational programs into the full school environment, and to review materials, assessment instruments, and testing practices, as well as staff selection procedures and staff development programs.

In conclusion, close cooperation and sincere and caring performance among federal and state educational agencies, communities, parents, and schools will improve children and youth's psychological and academic performance. At least, children and youth will learn more, teachers will be more fulfilled, and parents will feel better about their children and themselves. It follows, therefore, that educational agencies, the school, home, and community must engage in positive interactions. Parents, in particular, need to know not only the dramatics of the media, for example, but the more mundane, day-to-day significant activities of the school's function. More precisely, parents just simply need to be involved in school. And teachers and administration must have the security and faith to believe that the more parents are involved, the more they will understand and, thus, support the school. Besides, collaborative efforts on education are reflective of participatory communities. Community participation influences students' performance, thus the time spent with parents and students outside of the classroom, as well as teachers' involvement in school-community organizations and activities, will very probably result in better teaching and learning. In the face of the monumental U.S. educational dilemma, the pursuit of this model of participatory educational democracy should help create at least an approximation of what is herein conceptualized, developed, and presented for public consumption.

As a function of life, change must allow decision makers and significant others to make leaps into the unknown, to take risks and to mitigate risks. By examining and then trying the seemingly impossible, limits of the possible may be uncovered. This is possible if there is fundamental belief in the abilities of children and youth and the possibilities of parents helping more with children—all parents and all children. When educational agencies, parents, teachers, and administrators work together and are part of a comprehensive delivery system, students perform better socially and academically.

REFERENCES

Asche, J. (1989). *Handbook for principals and teachers: A collaborative approach for the effective involvement of community and business volunteers at the school site.* Alexandria, Virginia: National Association of Partners in Education.

Contreras, A. R. (1988). Use of educational reform to create effective schools. *Education and Urban Society, 20*(4), 399–413.

Koppman, P. S. (February/May, 1989). Recognizing the importance of parents. *Reading Today, 3*.

Nettles, S. M. (1991). Community involvement and disadvantaged students: A review. *Review of Educational Research, 61*(3), 379–406.

Stallings, J. (1986). What do we mean by quality in education. In English, F.W. et al. (Eds.), *Rethinking reform. The principal's dilemma* (pp. 61–70). Reston, Virginia: National Association of Secondary School Principals.

United States Bureau of the Census (1991). *The Hispanic population in the United States: March 1990.* (Current Population Report, Series P–20, No. 449). Washington, D.C.: Government Printing Office.

Williams, M. F. (1988). *Neighborhood organizing for urban school reform.* New York: Teachers College Press.

Chapter 12

ADVOCACY FOR SCHOOL AND HOME PARTNERSHIP

Numerous agencies, organizations, and associations in the public and private sectors advise educators and parents of the need to involve parents in the process of educating children. This chapter lists some of these organizations. Part one identifies organizations that have received national recognition for promoting the partnership between home and school. Part two presents a list of organizations that work with local educational communities and parents.

PART ONE: SELECTED ORGANIZATIONAL PROFILE

Advocates for Children of New York, Inc.
  24–16 Bridge Plaza South, Long Island City, NY 11101; (718) 729-8866

  A private, nonprofit organization concerned about the denial of equal education opportunity and due process safeguards to thousands of children in the New York City schools, Advocates for Children is a partnership of lawyers, advocates, counselors, parent trainers, and organizers that provides information and assistance to parents in protecting students' rights.

Asian American Communications
  Box 49, 525 West 120th St., New York, NY 10027; (212) 678-3260

Asian American Communications monitors educational policies, materials, and services for Asian American students; it also runs workshops and conducts seminars.

Aspira of America, Inc.
1112 16th St., NW, Suite 340, Washington, DC 20036; (202) 835-3600

Aspira's central mission is to advance the socio-economic development of the Latino community. To fulfill this mission, it has worked for 30 years to provide youth with the emotional, intellectual and practical resources they need to remain in school and to contribute to their community. Aspira is a nonprofit organization serving Puerto Rican and other Latino youth through leadership development and education. Aspira is the oldest and largest Hispanic youth organization in the United States.

Center for Collaborative Education
1573 Madison Ave., Room 412, New York, NY 10029; (212) 348-7821

The center is a joint project of six New York City public schools to promote a new approach to learning. By enhancing the visibility of its schools and assisting others who want to build or redesign schools, the center aims to build a network of public schools that teaches students to use their minds critically and purposefully.

Children's Defense Fund
122 C St., NW, Washington, D. C. 20001; (202) 628-8787

A national, nonprofit organization which exists to provide an effective voice for the children of America who cannot vote, lobby, or speak for themselves. The fund represents children's interests through research to document extent of problems; it also publishes reports and a national newsletter, *CDF Reports*, and sponsors an annual national conference.

Coalition of Essential Schools
Brown University, Box 1938, Providence, RI 02912; (401) 863-3384

The coalition is a high school-university partnership devoted to strengthening the learning of students by supporting each school's efforts to reform its priorities and simplify its structure. Each school develops a plan appropriate to its own setting but based on a simple set of shared principles that give focus to its efforts.

District Parent Council
527 Beech St., East Lansing, MI 48823

The District Parent Council is made up of representatives from each school in the district, plus a school board member. The council serves in an advisory role to the school board and as a communication link between school district and parents. One project it supports and sponsors is Positive Prevention, a parents' group focusing on drug education and drug abuse prevention.

ENLACE: Latino Children Educational Network
429 White Plains Rd., Bronx, NY 10473; (212) 636-6425

ENLACE: Latino Children Educational Network is a nonprofit organization established to help Latino children and youth by providing financial resources and educational opportunities through an educational network.

Family Resource Exchange
230 North Michigan Ave., Suite 1625, Chicago, IL 60601; (312) 726-4750

Family Resource Exchange is a national federation of more than 2,000 individuals and organizations promoting the development of prevention-oriented, community-based programs to strengthen families. It provides technical assistance and a wide variety of services on all aspects of program development; it also publishes books and reports, and sponsors conferences.

Friends of Compton Unified Students (FOCUS)
1515 West 155th St., Compton, CA 90220

This group of Hispanic parents is concerned about a number of discriminatory practices in the schools, such as Hispanic children not being chosen to participate in the gifted and talented program; the district not having enough programs to serve Latino students; and teachers being accused of verbal and physical abuse of Hispanic students. FOCUS sponsors marches and demonstrations to protest such instances of discrimination. It has also filed a lawsuit in Compton Superior Court, charging the district with failing to provide quality education for Hispanic children, and the teachers and administrators with discrimination against and verbal harassment of both students and parents.

Institute for Responsive Education
6005 Commonwealth Ave., Boston, MA 02215; (617) 353-3309

A nonprofit public interest research and advocacy organization, the institute promotes citizen participation in education for school improvement. In addition to research reports, it provides technical assistance, consultation, and policy development support. It also operates demonstration projects, especially in school-family-community links in low-income urban areas and publishes *Equity and Choice*.

Interface's Schoolwatch
666 Broadway, New York, NY 10012; (212) 674-2121

Interface's Schoolwatch is a program to promote more effective public schools. Schoolwatch activities include research on management and programs at the Board of Education and monitoring of school finances and policy implementation. A key part of Schoolwatch is the outreach program, which provides information, training, and technical assistance to parents, community-based organizations, and community school boards so that they can be effective partners in local school improvement.

Mexican American Legal Defense and Education Fund (MALDEF)
634 S. Spring St., 11th Floor, Los Angeles, CA 90014

MALDEF is a national civil rights organization formed 20 years ago to assist Latino parents and citizens. One of its current aims is to increase Latino parental involvement in a meaningful way, in order to promote partnership and accountability so that the children receive the benefits of a better education. It provides training for Latino parents through workshops on how to work with teachers, monitor their children's academic progress, find out about special programs offered by the school, and solve problems their children may be having in school.

National Association of Partners in Education, Inc.
601 Wythe St., Suite 200, Alexandria, VA 22314; (703) 836-4880

This organization represents the many schools, businesses, community groups, educators, and individual volunteers working together as partners to enhance the education of children. It publishes monthly and quarterly newsletters for members, offers program development training, and sponsors several conferences throughout the year.

National Black Child Development Institute
1463 Rhode Island Ave., NW, Washington, DC 20005; (202) 387-1281

This is a national, nonprofit, educational organization established to improve the quality of life for black children and youth. The institute focuses on issues of child care and child welfare, health, and education. It publishes reports, a quarterly newsletter, *The Black Child Advocate*, and *Child Health Talk;* and also sponsors a national conference.

National Committee for Citizens in Education (NCCE)
10840 Little Patuxent Parkway, Suite 301, Columbia, MD 21044; (301) 977-9300

The NCCE is a nonprofit organization dedicated to increasing citizen involvement in the affairs of the nation's public schools. NCCE is a successor to the National Committee for Support of the Public Schools founded in 1962 by Agnes Meyer, Harry Truman, and others. The original organization concentrated on increased federal assistance to public education. In 1973, the committee reorganized, took its new name, and reconstituted its purpose. NCCE has conducted hearings across the United States on who controls America's public schools, taking testimony from hundreds of individuals and organizations.

National Council of la Raza (NCLR)
810 First St. NE, Suite 300, Washington, DC 20002-4205; (202) 289-1380

NCLR is a nonprofit organization incorporated in Arizona in 1968. It serves as an advocate for Hispanic Americans and as a national umbrella organization for about 100 formal affiliates and community-based groups that serve 32 states, Puerto Rico, and the District of Columbia, and for other local Hispanic organizations nationwide. The NCLR is governed by a 29-member board of directors that reflects the varied Hispanic population in terms of subgroups and regional representation, and half the elected board members represent council affiliates or other constituencies. The council works extensively in coalitions with other Hispanic, minority, and mainstream organizations both on specific issues, such as education or housing, and on broader-scope efforts.

The National Parent Teachers Association (PTA)
700 Rush St., Chicago, IL 60611-2571; (312) 787-0977

The PTA is a volunteer association seeking to unite home, school, and community in promoting the education, health, and safety of children, youth, and families. It serves as a resource center and can supply information on many topics; it also publishes *PTA Today*, and a newsletter about federal legislative issues affecting children and youth.

Advocacy for School and Home Partnership 225

National Urban League
   500 East 62nd St., New York, NY 10021; (212) 310-9000

   The National Urban League is an inter-racial, nonprofit community service organization using the tools and methods of social work, economics, law, and business management to secure equal opportunities in all sectors of American society for black Americans and other minorities. It uses direct services, research, advocacy, and bridge building. It fosters the development of community-based educational programs to improve the academic achievement of minority students.

Options
   P. O. Box 788, Milford, PA 18337

   Options, an organization of parents and teachers of students in special education, was founded in May 1991. Its purpose is to assist parents in guiding these children through their educational careers. It has sponsored speakers and workshops on state regulations for special education, and on how to develop a cooperative relationship between parents and schools.

Parents Coalition for Education in New York City, Inc.
   24–16 Bridge Plaza South, Long Island City, NY 11101;
   (718) 729-8866

   The coalition is a broadly multi-ethnic citywide parents membership organization that supports parents' participation in decision making at social, school, district, and citywide levels.

Student Advocacy, Inc.
   172 S. Broadway, White Plains, NY 10605

   Student Advocacy is a project sponsored and funded by the Youth Bureau and Department of Social Services in New York's Westchester, Rockland, and Putnam counties. Its purpose is to help Hispanic parents learn how the educational system works and what they can do to make sure their children receive a quality education. Assistance and support are available for children in special education, those with limited English proficiency, and students with attendance and behavior problems. Translators, interpreters, mediators, and advocates are available to help parents become more involved and to assert their rights.

PART TWO: ORGANIZATIONAL DIRECTORY

Adults for Children's
　Education (ACE)
　RFD, Box 658
　Madison, ME 04950

Association for Community-
　Based Education
　1806 Vernon St. NW
　Washington, DC 20009
　(202) 462-6333

Big Apple Parent's Paper
　928 Broadway
　Suite 709
　New York, NY 10010
　(212) 533-2277

Bladen County Board of
　Education, Chapter 1
　P. O. Box 37
　Elizabeth Town, NC 28337

Carnegie Corporation
　437 Madison Ave.
　New York, NY 10022
　(212) 371-3200

Center for Community
　Education
　School of Social Work
　Rutgers–The State
　University of New Jersey
　Kilmer Campus
　Bldg. 4087
　New Brunswick, NJ 08903
　(201) 932-3367

Centro de Estudios
　Puertoriquenos
　Hunter College of the City
　University of New York
　695 Park Ave.
　New York, NY 10021

Chicago Panel on Public
　School Policy and Finance
　202 South State St.
　Suite 1212
　Chicago, IL 60604

Children Are Precious, Inc.
　1668 Zerega Ave.
　Bronx, NY 10462
　(212) 863-1880

Advocacy for School and Home Partnership

Cities in Schools
    1023 15th Street NW
    Suite 600
    Washington, DC 20001
    (202) 861-0230

Citizens Committee for
    Children of New York, Inc.
    105 East 22nd St.
    New York, NY 10010
    (212) 673-1800

Citizens of Albany for
    Responsible Education
    (CARE)
    177 S. Manning Blvd.
    Albany, NY 12208

Clearinghouse on Adult
    Education
    U. S. Department of
    Education
    400 Maryland Ave. SW
    Room 44
    Mail Stop 7240
    Washington, DC 20202
    (202) 732-2396

Community Association of
    Progressive Dominicans,
    Inc.
    2268 Amsterdam Ave.
    New York, NY
    (212) 740-3866

Community Resource
    Exchange
    17 Murray St.
    New York, NY 10007
    (212) 349-8155

Community Service Society
    (CSS)
    105 E. 22nd St.
    New York, NY 10010
    (212) 614-5352

Concerned Parent
    Group 137A
    RR2 Box
    Livonia, MO 63551

Council for Basic Education
    725 15th St. NW
    Washington, DC 20005

Denver Council
    PTSA
    772 Marion St.
    Denver, CO 80218

Designs for Change
    220 South State St.
    Chicago, IL 60604
    (312) 922-0317

Education Advisory
    2267 Kizcare
    West Vancouver
    British Columbia
    Canada, V7V2C1

Educational Excellence
    Network
    1112 16th St. NW
    Suite 500
    Washington, DC 20036
    (202) 785-2985

Educational Priorities Panel
    105 E. 22nd St.
    New York, NY 10010
    (212) 614-5317

Edwin Gould Foundation for
  Children
  23 Gramercy Park South
  New York, NY 10003
  (212) 982-5200

ERIC Clearinghouse on Adult
  Career and Vocational
  Education
  Cherry A. McGell Banks
  144 Railroad Ave.
  Suite 107
  1900 Kenny Road
  Columbus, OH 43210
  (800) 848-4815

Family Matters Project
  Cornell University
  7 Research Park
  Ithaca, NY 14850
  (607) 255-2260

Family Resource Coalition
  200 North Michigan Ave.
  Suite 1625
  Chicago, IL 60601

Ford Foundation
  320 E. 43rd St.
  New York, NY 10017
  (212) 573-5000

Foundation for Child
  Development
  345 E. 46th St.
  Room 700
  New York, NY 10017
  (212) 697-3100

Fund for the City of New York
  121 Ave. of the Americas
  6th Fl.
  New York, NY 10013
  (212) 698-1240

Fund for New York City
  Public Education
  96 Morton St.
  9th Floor
  New York, NY 10014
  (212) 645-5110

Harvard Family Research
  Project
  Harvard Graduate School
  of Education
  301 Gutman Library,
  Appian Way
  Cambridge, MA 02138
  (617) 495-9108

Hasbro Foundation for
  Children
  32 W. 23rd St.
  New York, NY 10010
  (212) 645-2400

Heckscher Foundation for
  Children
  17 E. 47th St.
  New York, NY 10017
  (212) 371-7735

Hermandad Mexicana
  Nacional
  1115 59 Sherman Way
  North Hollywood, CA
  91605
  (818) 764-9965

Hispanic Policy Development
  Project
  250 Park Ave. South
  Suite 500A
  New York, NY 10003
  (212) 529-9323

Advocacy for School and Home Partnership

Home and School Institute, Inc.
1201 16th Street NW
Washington, DC 20036
(202) 466-3633

Lafayette Citizens for Public Education (CPED)
P. O. Box 5153
Lafayette, LA 70502

Minnesota Hispanic Education Program, Inc.
245 E. 6th St.
Suite 706
St. Paul, MN 55901
(612) 222-6014

National Alliance of Black School Educators (NABSE)
2816 Georgia Ave.
Washington, DC 20001
(212) 483-1549

National Association for Asian and Pacific American Education
c/o ARC Associates Inc.
310 Eighth St.
Suite 301
Oakland, CA 94607

National Association for Family Day Care
725 15th St. NW, Suite 505
Washington, DC 20005
(202) 347-3356

National Association for the Advancement of Colored People (NAACP)
Project Excellence
260 Fifth Ave.
6th Floor
New York, NY 10001-6408
(212) 481-4100

National Clearinghouse on Literacy Education
1118 22a St. NW
Washington, DC 20037
(202) 429-9292

National Coalition for Parent Involvement in Education
Box 39 National Education Association
1201 16th St., NW
Washington, DC 20036
(202) 822-7015

National Coalition of Advocates for Children
100 Boston St.
Suite 737
Boston, MA 02116
(617) 357-8507

National Education Association (NEA)
1201 16th St. NW
Washington, DC 20036
(202) 833-4000

National Head Start Association
1280 King St.
Suite 200
Alexandria, VA 22314

National Korean American
 Parents Council
 42-31 149th St.
 Flushing, NY 11355
 (718) 539-9658

Page Parents for Education
 112 Poplar St.
 Franklin, TN 37064

Parent Advocacy Coalition for
 Educational Rights
 (PACER)
 4826 Chicago Ave. South
 Minneapolis, MN 55417-1055
 (612) 827-2966

Parent Co-operative
 Elementary Program
 P. O. Box 1602
 Lynnwood, WA 98046

Parenting Programs
 Department of Health
 Education/Community
 Affairs
 North Shore University
 Hospital
 300 Community Dr.
 Manhasset, NY 11030
 (516) 562-3045

Parenting Resource Center
 1096 Park Ave.
 Suite 1B
 New York, NY 10028

Parent Leadership Project
 City University of New
 York
 John Jay College of
 Criminal Justice
 899 Tenth Ave.
 New York, NY 10019
 (212) 237-8000

Parent Resource Center
 121 Sixth Ave., 6th Floor
 New York, NY 10013
 (212) 925-6675

Parents Educational Network
 (PEN)
 P. O. Box 27223
 El Jobean, FL 33927

Parents Organizing to
 Improve School and
 Education (POISE)
 Pt. 1 Box 35N-1
 Crescent, OK 73028

Parents Union for Public
 Schools in Philadelphia
 401 North Broad St.
 Suite 895
 Philadelphia, PA 19108

Project Choice
 Chinese Opportunities in
 Career Education
 350 Grant St.
 Room 512
 New York, NY 10002

Puerto Rican/Latino
   Education Roundtable
   c/o Center for Puerto Rican
   Studies
   Hunter College
   695 Park Ave.
   New York, NY 10021
   (212) 772-5691

Research for Better Schools
   444 North Third St.
   Philadelphia, PA 19123-4107
   (215) 574-9300

Rockefeller Foundation
   1133 Ave. of the Americas
   New York, NY 10036

Single Parent Network Inc.
   P. O. Box 1072
   Chelsea Station
   New York, NY 10011

United Parents Association of
   New York City
   70 Lafayette St.
   New York, NY 10013
   (212) 619-0095

Urban Appalachian Council
   2115 W. 8th St.
   Cincinnati, OH 45204

Woodlands Mountain
   Institute
   Box 907
   Franklin, WV 26807

Yale University Child Study
   Center
   230 South Frontage Rd
   P. O. Box 3333
   New Haven, CT 06510

AUTHOR INDEX

Adams, D., 130
Ahlbrandt, R. S., 117
Andrews, R., 144, 146, 148
Angus, I., 7
Anrig, G. R., 185
Appel, K., 74
Apple, M., 3
Arnez, N. L., 128
Asante, M. K., 7
Asche, J., 141, 142, 146, 148, 213, 215
Aspira Association, 161

Baecher, R., 152
Banks, J. A., 79
Barth, R., 85
Bastiani, J., 182, 200
Battle, J., 120
Beal, A. V., 179, 189
Beane, J. A., 131
Behn, R. D., 6
Bell, T., 177
Bennett, C. T., 24
Bennett, K. P., 71, 73, 86
Bennett, W. L., 82
Berger, J., 26, 27, 187, 189, 200

Bickerton, D., 13
Bilingual Education Act, 154
Bill, R. E., 124
Billingsley, A., 128
Bizar, M., 162, 163
Bloom, A., 7
Bloom, B., 123, 124
Bloom, B. S., 160, 162, 163, 171
Boles, R., 132
Branden, N., 120, 128
Breivogel, W. F., 99
Brewer, J., 13
Briggs, D., 132
Briles, J., 121
Bronfenbrenner, U., 69, 130
Brophy, J., 119, 170, 171
Burke, F. G., ix
Butler, H. F., 13

Campbell, E. Q. *See* Coleman, J.
Campbell, F., 9
Canfield, J., 120

233

Capizzi-Snipper, G., 163, 165
Carino, B. V., 51, 56
Carrasquillo, A., 35, 36, 38, 40, 42, 45, 152, 153, 154
Carter, T., 25
Center for Population Options, 4
Chan, K. S., 5
Chavkin, N. F., ix, 103, 176, 183
Chen, C. S., 60
Cheng, L. L., 52, 64
Chu-Chang, M., 52, 54, 60
Clark, A., 175
Cochran, M., 128, 130, 176, 177, 189
Cohen, R., 13
Coleman, J., 72, 76, 84, 88, 161, 176
Comer, J., 177, 179, 183, 185, 187
Contreras, A. R., 141, 142, 146, 148, 153, 214, 215
Cooley, C. H., 115, 131
Coopersmith, R. L., 132
Coopersmith, S., 128
Craig, D. R., 13
Crawford, J., 152, 154
Cremin, L. A., 70, 84
Cronin, J., 99
Cross, D., 98
Cummins, J., 150, 152, 153, 154, 159, 161, 165

Dantley, B., 24
Davies, D., 71, 72, 179, 183, 185, 188
Davis, C., 35, 38
Davis, D., 125
Deci, E. L., 124
Denzin, N. K., 25
DePalmer, A., 16
Deutsch, C. H., 25
Dewey, J., 70, 72, 115, 116
Diop, C. A., 14
Doebla, C. H., 99
Dorsey-Gaines, C., ix
Douglas, M., 16
Dulney, K. H., ix, 130, 175, 176, 177

Edelman, M. W., 5
Edmonds, R. R., 159, 161
Epstein, J. C. L., 176, 178, 185, 200
Espenshad, T., 18
Evans, K. M., 70, 71, 123

Fantini, M., 114
Farber, A., 129
Fawcet, J. T., 51, 56
Felt, J. C., 51, 53, 55, 56, 57
Feris, W. H., 13, 14
Filipczak, J., 89
First, J. M., x
Fitzpatrick, J., 41
Fraenkel, G., 13
Froebenius, L., 14

Garbarino, J., 124
Gardner, B., 16
General Accounting Office., 56
Getzels, J. W., 69, 76, 88
Gibb, J., 114
Gibbons, M., 119
Gifford, B., 97
Ginot, H. G., 120
Glaser, R., 119
Glasser, W., 114
Goetz, J. P., 71
Good, T., 170, 171
Goodman, K., 167
Gordon, I. J., 99
Gordon, T., 120
Gottfresdon, G. D., 142, 148, 149
Gough, P. B., 84, 176
Graubard, S. R., x
Greene, D., 124, 125

Hailer, R., 99
Hale-Benson, J. H., 14, 26
Haley, B., 6
Hallman, H. W., 117
Hanson, S., 121
Haskins, J., 13
Hayes, C. D., 4
Heath, S. B., 180
Heleen, O., 176, 180, 181, 185
Henderson, A. T., 72, 99, 100, 128, 130, 159, 161, 171, 172, 176, 177, 185, 200

Henderson, C., 128, 130, 176, 177, 189
Herber, R., 9
Herskovits, M. J., 13
Hill, R. B., 22
Hirsch, E. D., 3, 7, 164
Hobbs, N., 71
Hobson, C. J. *See* Coleman, J.
Hofferth, S. L., 4
Hoge, R., 121
Howe, L. W., 114
Howe, M. M., 114
Huefner, D. S., 177, 187, 188, 200, 201, 203
Hyde, A., 162, 163
Hymes, D., 14

Ignacio, L. F., 51, 52
Ingster, B., 128
Institute for Puerto Rican Policy, 37, 38

Jacobson, L., 122
James, G. M., 14
Jersild, A. T., 122, 132
Jhally, S., 7
Johnston, M., 84, 185, 200

Kagan, S. L., 176, 182
Kellogg, J. B., 18
Kerr, B. A., 132
Keto, C. T., 13
Kierstead, F. D., 60
Kinder, J. H., 176, 182, 183, 190

Kleiber, D. A., 124
Knowles, L. L., 19, 20
Koppman, P. S., 210
Krasnow, J. H., 176, 180, 181, 185
Kritz, M., 38
Kroth, R. L., 200

Ladson, G., x
Laosa, L., 176
Leavitt, J., 38
Le Compte, M. D., 71, 73, 86
Leitcher, H. J., 74, 77
Lepper, M. R., 124, 125
Levy, E., 13, 17, 131
Lipker, R. P., 131
Lippett, R., 114
London, C. B. G., 16, 18
Lovecky, D. V., 132

McAdoo, H. P., 19, 22, 28
McDaniel, T. R., 121, 124
McFarland, R., 128
McFee, O. D., x
McLaren, D. L., 24
McPortland, J. See Coleman, J.
Maehr, M. L., 124
Marquet, J., 14
Marshall, C. A., 29
Martinez-Perez, L., 132
Maslow, A. H., 116
Mattox, B., 85
Melargno, R., 101
Mischel, W., 119

Mood, A. M. See Coleman, J.
Moore, J. L., 36, 37, 38
Mortimore, P., 144, 150
Muller, T., 18

National Committee for Citizens in Education, 87, 92, 142, 143, 148
National Council of la Raza, 40
National Governors' Association, 71
Nedler, S. E., x
Neiser, U., 5
Nelms, C., 99
Nettles, S. M., 141, 171, 172, 211, 213, 215
New York State Education Department, 82, 84, 89
Nobles, N., 13, 14, 29

Ogbu, L. U., 5, 7
O'Hare, W. P., 51, 53, 55, 56, 57
Orum, L. S., 36, 44, 45
Otto, H. G., 42

Pachón, H., 36, 37, 38
Pai, Y., 5, 7
Parsons, T., 72, 76, 77
Patterson, O., 26
Pentecoste, J., 99
Perkins, U. E., 5
Perrone, P., 132
Phillips, G., 119

Author Index

Prewitt, K., 19, 20
Pysykowski, I. S., 101, 176

Ravitch, D., 13, 16
Reckinger, N., 126
Renaldo, J., 13, 17, 131
Reudan, R., 5
Rich, D., 76, 85, 88, 176, 187
Richards, D., 13
Rioux, W., 185
Rogers, J. A., 14
Rogler, L. A., 129
Rosenthal, R., 122
Rothenberg, P., 5
Rothman, R., 117
Rowell, J. C., 99
Ryan, C., 100

Sammons, P., 144, 150
Samuels, S. C., 120, 121
Schaps, E., 83, 87
Schindler-Raiman, E., 114
Schmuck, P. A., 119
Schmuck, R. A., 119
Scholl, G. T., 200
Schutz, N. C., 114
Scobie, R., 119
Scott-Jones, D., 142, 149
Seeley, D. S., 99
Shavelson, R., 132
Sigel, L., 176
Silber, J., 83
Slaughter, D., 9
Slotnik, J., 84, 185, 200

Smith, E., 121
Smith, F., 167
Sobol, T., 84, 86
Solomon, D., 83, 87
Sonnier, I. L., 88, 130
Sowell, T., 13, 17, 18
Spring, J., 70, 73, 82, 92, 176, 180, 182, 183, 184
Stack, C., 29
Stafford, L., 101
Stallings, J., 214
Stanford Research Institute, 85
Stevenson, H. W., 60
Strom, N. T., 101
Sudarkasa, N., 13, 29, 30
Swap-McAllister, S., 177, 185, 187, 200
Swedo, J., 170

Taylor, D. ix
Todd, T. D., 179, 180, 189, 190
Topping, K. J., 131
Trotter, R. J., 86

Ungar, M. S., 84
United Federation of Teachers Bulletin, 130
United States Bureau of the Census, ix, 36, 37, 38, 39, 40, 52, 56, 152, 207
United States Department of Education, 149, 160

United States Department of Health and Human Services, 4

Valdivieso, R., 35, 38
Valdman, A., 13
Valentine, C., 26
Vanderslice, V., 102
Van Dien, J., 85
Van Sertima, I., 13
Vaupel, R. D., 6

Walburg, H. J., 80, 84, 88, 189
Weber, M., 70, 72, 77
Wei, T.T.D., 58
Weiler, K., 72, 80, 84
Weinfeld, F. D. *See* Coleman, J.

Weinstein, G., 114
Wells, A. S., 177, 188, 200
Wells, G., 163, 165, 166, 167, 172
Welsh, C. E., 5
Wiley, D., 16
Wilkerson, D. A., 100
Williams, J. D., 163, 165
Williams, L., 5
Williams, M. F., 213, 215
Wilson, J., 99
Woo, J.W.T., 52, 53, 55, 58, 60

Yao, L., ix, 60
Yeakey, C. C., 24
York, R. L. *See* Coleman, J.
Young, T. R., 128

SUBJECT INDEX

African Americans
  Africentric People, 14
  Definition, 13
  Family Status, 20–27
Asians
  Chinese, 53–54
  Educational Style, 60–64
  Family, 57–60
  Filipino, 55
  Immigration, 51–53, 55–57
  Japanese, 54
  Koreans, 54–55
  Parental Involvement, 64–66
  Students, 60–64
  Status, 56–57

Bilingual Education, 154

Community, 69–71, 74–76, 78–79
Co-oping Model, 200–203
Cultural Literacy, 164–165

Empowerment
  Definition, 102–103

English as a second language, 154–155

Family Structure, 3–10

Hispanics
  Central and South Americans, 38
  Cubans, 37
  Definition, 35–36
  Dominicans, 37–38
  Family, 41–43
  Mexicans, 36
  Puerto Ricans, 37
  Status, 36–40

National Parents Organizations, 208–210, 219–231

Parental Involvement, ix, x, 43, 84–89, 131–132, 171–172, 175–188, 214–218
Parental Network, 89–91

Parent Associations. *See* National Parents Organizations.
Parent Councils, 91–92
Parent-Teacher Relationships, 188–198
Public Schooling, 73–74

School, 84–88, 141–142
   Climate, 142, 145–146
   Leadership, 146–148
   Learning, 150–162
   Parents' Roles, 155–156

School Boards, 79–82, 210–214
School Districts, 79–80
Self Concept, 113–116, 120–121, 123–130, 132–136
Sensitivity, 118–120
Students, 116–118
   Attendance, 145
   Interaction, 171
   Limited English Proficient, 152–153
   Performance, 121–122
   Readiness, 130–131, 159–161, 170

SOURCE BOOKS ON EDUCATION

1. Bilingual Education: *A Source Book for Educators*, by Alba N. Ambert and Sarah Melendez
2. Reading and Study Skills in the Secondary Schools: *A Source Book*, by Joyce N. French
3. Creating Connections: *Books, Kits, and Games for Children*, by Betty P. Cleaver, Barbara Chatton, and Shirley Vittum Morrison
4. Gifted, Talented, and Creative Young People: *A Guide to Theory, Teaching, and Research*, by Morris I. Stein
5. Teaching Science to Young Children: *A Resource Book*, by Mary D. Iatridis
6. Microcomputers and Social Studies: *A Resource Guide for the Middle and Secondary Grades*, by Joseph A. Braun, Jr.
7. Special Education: *A Source Book*, by Manny Sternlicht
8. Computers in the Classroom... What Shall I Do? *A Guide*, by Walter Burke
9. Learning to Read and Write: The Role of Language Acquisition and Aesthetic Development, *A Resource Guide*, by Ellen J. Brooks
10. School Play: *A Source Book*, by James H. Block and Nancy R. King
11. Computer Simulations: *A Source Book to Learning in an Electronic Environment*, by Jerry Willis, Larry Hovey, and Kathleen Hovey
12. Day Care: *A Source Book*, by Kathleen Pullan Watkins and Lucius Durant, Jr.
13. Project Head Start: *Past, Present, and Future Trends in the Context of Family Needs*, by Valora Washington and Ura Jean Oyemade
14. Adult Literacy: *A Source Book and Guide*, by Joyce French
15. Mathematics Education in Secondary Schools and Two-Year Colleges: *A Source Book*, by Louise S. Grinstein and Paul J. Campbell
16. Black Children and American Institutions: *An Ecological Review and Resource Guide*, by Valora Washington and Velma LaPoint
17. Resources for Educational Equity: *A Source Book for Grades Pre-Kindergarten–12*, by Merle Froschl and Barbara Sprung
18. Multicultural Education: *A Source Book*, by Patricia G. Ramsey, Edwina Battle Vold, and Leslie R. Williams
19. Sexuality Education: *A Resource Book*, by Carol Cassell and Pamela M. Wilson
20. Reforming Teacher Education: *Issues and New Directions*, edited by Joseph A. Braun, Jr.
21. Educational Technology: *Planning and Resource Guide Supporting Curriculum*, by James E. Eisele and Mary Ellin Eisele
22. Critical Issues in Foreign Language Instruction, edited by Ellen S. Silber
23. The Education of Women in the United States: *A Guide to Theory, Teaching, and Research*, by Averil Evans McClelland
24. Materials and Strategies for the Education of Trainable Mentally Retarded Learners, by James P. White
25. Rural Education: *Issues and Practice*, by Alan J. DeYoung
26. Educational Testing: *Issues and Applications*, by Kathy E. Green
27. The Writing Center: *New Directions*, edited by Ray Wallace and Jeanne Simpson
28. Teaching Thinking Skills: *Theory and Practice*, by Joyce N. French and Carol Rhoder

29. Teaching Social Studies to the Young Child: *A Research and Resource Guide*, by Blythe S. Farb Hinitz
30. Telecommunications: *A Handbook for Educators*, by Reza Azarmsa
31. Catholic School Education in the United States: *Development and Current Concerns*, by Mary A. Grant and Thomas C. Hunt
32. Day Care: *A Source Book,* Second Edition, by Kathleen Pullan Watki and Lucius Durant, Jr.
33. School Principals and Change, by Michael D. Richardson, Paula M. Short, and Robert L. Prickett
34. Play in Practice: *A Systems Approach to Making Good Play Happen,* edited by Karen VanderVen, Paul Niemiec, and Roberta Schomburg
35. Teaching Science to Children, Second Edition, by Mary D. Iatridis with a contribution by Miriam Marecek
36. Kits, Games and Manipulatives for the Elementary School Classroom: *A Source Book,* by Andrea Hoffman and Ann Glannon
37. Parents and Schools: *A Source Book,* by Angela Carrasquillo and Clement B. G. London
38. Project Head Start: *Models and Strategies for the Twenty-First Century,* by Valora Washington and Ura Jean Oyemade Bailey
39. Instrumentation in Education: *An Anthology,* by Lloyd Bishop and Paula E. Lester